The Sharecroppers

Denisa Nickell Hanania

D1069325

PRESS

The Sharecroppers
by Denisa Nickell Hanania

Printed in the United States of America

ISBN 9781628399622

Unless otherwise indicated, Bible quotations are taken from The King James Version of the Bible.

www.xulonpress.com

ALSO BY DENISA NICKELL HANANIA

A Talent to Deceive

(Avalon Press)

The Sharecroppers is dedicated to
my great-grandparents, Mary and Charley Crouse;
my grandparents, Ortha and Leonard Scott;
and my parents, Esther and Kendall Nickell.
Thank you for blessing me with such a beautiful heritage.
I am forever grateful.

Acknowledgements

T hank you to my cherished aunts and uncles for sharing your life stories with me. You have been so kind, patiently answering my endless questions. Thank you for having faith that I would eventually finish writing. Delphia and Carroll Waddell, Bernece and John Ellis, Bernard and Linda Crouse, Delora and Edward Brown, Rachel and Dallas Hensley, Earl and Dewdrop Crouse, Ernest and Diane Crouse, Wes and Vermel Crouse, Ella Marie and John Smith, and Chester Crouse, you lived *The Sharecroppers*.

A special thank you to my husband, Marwan Hanania, and our boys, Dan, Max, Elijah, Caleb, Nick, and Tommy, who sacrificed much of my attention and took over my responsibilities so that I could finish this book. Good news. I'm thinking about taking up cooking again—but probably not laundry.

Much loving gratitude to my readers Daniel Hendon and Carla Pelfrey. Thank you for your enthusiasm, your encouragement, and your valuable feedback. You are both continual blessings in my life.

A special thank you to Arkansas Historian, Donna Brewer Jackson. No one knows the history of Mississippi County better than you do. Thank you for opening the Depot museum just for me, pulling out volume after volume of relevant materials, and even sharing your own extensive personal research. I especially appreciate your reading through my manuscript and checking for historical accuracy.

Thank you to Professor Frances S. Fendler, JD, for sharing your father's memoirs with me and allowing me to fictionalize Oscar Fendler's story.

Thank you to each of my friends and family who encouraged and prayed for me as I wrote. This journey has been made all the sweeter by your belief in me.

Much appreciation to my editor, Carla Stoneberg. You have an incredible knowledge of written and oral language. You audited my manuscript, not just looking for misplaced commas, but also making sure the words and phrases I used were consistent with how people would have talked in the years of the story. Thank you, Carla. I am so grateful!

With much gratitude to God for all the Grace He pours out on me

Prologue

For those of you whose roots grow deep in cotton soil, a legacy calls you back. The dirt whispers a name, echoing from a time when all that existed in the world happened right outside your door. It was where your life began, and to where your heart returns.

Life back then had the fullness of busy days without the rush. Days were predictable in routine, rich in value: chores, breakfast, choppin' cotton, dinner time, choppin' cotton, supper time, chores, then head off to bed. Half day on Saturday and nobody worked on Sunday.

Sharecroppers lived life in harmony with the seasons. The sun ordained the family's rising and their setting. The growing season determined whether school was in session and if your folks let you go. No one ate watermelon in June because they understood the time spent waiting would make the red fruit that much sweeter in August.

Cold nights were refreshing when you were tucked in between a fat, feather mattress and three patchwork quilts. Sleep came with the security of knowing city lights were too far away to fade your own view of heaven.

The modern concept of "family time" was unheard of. It was *all* family time. Everybody worked together; everyone was needed. Chores weren't proof your parents were abusing you. They were your function within the family. Even the smallest sharecropping children understood they played a part in harvesting enough cotton to buy what couldn't be raised in the garden. It was an annual contest, and there wasn't a farm boy around who didn't brag about how much cotton he could pick in a day's time.

Family entertainment meant humid evenings on the front porch when your uncles told tales so funny even the bull frogs chuckled. If you were a smart kid, you'd stay quiet so they'd forget you were there. Then you'd hear the really good stories.

Sharecropping parents didn't worry about self-esteem. They knew anybody would feel good about getting that much work done. Kids did their chores because doing so made their own lives easier. They remembered to feed the mule 'cause, come spring, they didn't want to push that plow themselves.

Nobody felt compelled to be environmentally responsible. The family kept a compost pile because natural fertilizer grows bigger, tastier vegetables. They threw their scraps in the pen because plumper hens serve up better fried chicken. You ate everything on your plate not because kids were starving in China, but because you'd worked up an appetite in the field.

Mississippi County, Arkansas, calls you back to a place where you are known — not by what you did last year, but by what you did when you were ten, and by what your grandparents did when they were ten. Small town reputations never die; they are simply reborn in the next generation. At family reunions you revert to all the ages you have ever been and hasten to a few you have yet to be.

Cross the county line and your heart is hand tuned to its own personal history. Past and present merge. Property divisions are marked by a grove of trees, a ditch, or a change in crop. Never mind that old Mr. Duckett has been resting under a walnut tree in the Manila cemetery for over thirty years. To you, that acreage on the south side of Highway 18 still belongs to him. Everywhere you look you see shadows of an age before cell phones, texting, and Play Station IV, a time when the idea of virtual baseball would have been laughed out of town.

How could video games beat playing *Grab the Fence*? Do you remember? Kids joined hands standing perpendicular to an electrical fence. At an unexpected moment, the first boy grabbed the live wire, sending a shock through the line of bodies and depositing its full force on the child at the end. It was great fun until your mother found out. And even she calmed down after the whuppin'.

"Knee high by the Fourth of July." That's how oldtimers used to tell if a crop was on target for a bumper year. Now farmers plant early corn, late corn, even mid-season corn. Seems almost disrespectful. It's gotten so a returning traveler isn't sure whether to be amazed at the corn's growth or to shake his head in dire prediction.

Many a boy and girl have moved on from the small farm towns that nurtured them. Others, like old Miz Hartmann, have lived over nine decades in the same county. Her years have been distinguished by the size of the crop, the cost of cotton seed, and the number of levy breaks along the Mississippi. Women, such as Marina Hartmann, have seasoned like the hardwood forests of Big Lake.

"Granny, if you could live anywhere on earth, where would you live?" her great-granddaughter once asked her.

"Why, right here in Manila," Miz Hartmann answered, as surprised by the question as the girl had been by her answer. Along with the rich soil that allowed them to feed their children, Mississippi County outlined the dreams she and Jake had spent their lives pursuing.

Miz Hartmann's eyes saw sights not even cataracts could dim. Her mind was filled with images of Jake, the children, Hattie, Doc, even little Oscar Fendler. That "runaway baby," as Marina called him, did pretty well for himself, went to Harvard and became a big city lawyer over in Blytheville.

Marina remembered maneuvering a mule and wagon down the road before it was paved. Surely old Right Hand Stumpy Road is better off without all those tree trunks sticking up, hindering the mules, forcing the wagon to mark a zigzag path to town. Modernization has brought progress, but it has also served up a less interesting ride. Perhaps that's true of more than just the roads.

Rice and soybeans have taken over much of Arkansas' cotton fields. Even for those who were raised here, memories of choppin' cotton under a blistering sun have faded like red paint off a weather-battered old barn. What is left is the knowledge that our lives are part of a good harvest. The birthright is in us still to be passed on. Some call it the heritage of the sharecroppers.

Denisa Hanania
September 16, 2013

Chapter One

November 1912

Manila, Arkansas

"There goes that runaway baby again!" Marina gasped. Hiking up her skirts to ankle length with one hand and holding onto her hat with the other, she took off running down South Dewey Avenue.

Bewildered, Jake stood still for a moment before he realized Marina was chasing a baby. The toddler was moving on all fours as fast as his little body could carry him. Hampered by his slowness to comprehend the situation, Jake caught up with Marina just as she scooped the little boy up into her arms.

The two-and-a-half-year-old giggled gleefully, oblivious to the grime that coated his play suit. "Look at you. You're a mess!" Marina chided, shaking her long, chestnut-colored curls into his face so they would tickle his nose.

"So are you," Jake observed.

Looking down the front of her dress, she realized her clothes were caked with dirt. "Well, I guess I am, but I couldn't very well leave him to find his own way home." Marina's head barely topped Jake's shoulder, so she had to look up. "Jake Hartmann, may I present Oscar Fendler, also known as Manila, Arkansas', infamous runaway baby."

"He's a pretty big-sized boy to be crawlin," Jake commented. "Can't he walk?"

"Yes, but not as fast as he can crawl." Marina was still out of breath. "Did you ever see a baby move so quick?"

Jake shook his head. "Where was he going?"

Marina pointed down the road to the Manila Stave Mill. "My guess is he wanted to jump in that sawdust pile down at the end of the street."

"How would a baby know there's a sawdust pile down there?"

"Oh, it's his favorite place to play." Her blue eyes danced. "He heads straight for it anytime he gets loose."

"How often is that?" Jake asked, clearly concerned that a two-year-old was crawling down the streets of Manila.

"At least once a week. More when he can manage it."

Jake shook his head in disgust. "What kind of a mother does he have?"

"A very good one, as a matter of fact," Marina assured him. "Mrs. Fendler spends all day helping her husband in his shop. Poor woman had malaria and typhoid fever last year. She was

18

about done in. She tries to keep a close eye on Oscar, but this little baby is just too fast, aren't you, honey?"

"You'll be a good mother someday," Jake observed.

Marina blushed and turned to walk back east on South Dewey Avenue. "I'd better get Oscar home before Mrs. Fendler panics. Now, what were you saying before Oscar crawled into town?"

Thrown by the abrupt change in conversation, Jake stammered. "The fair is coming to town in a couple of weeks, and I wondered if you might like to go with me."

Marina buried her face in Oscar's baby curls so Jake couldn't see her delight. "Why, yes. That would be fine. If you'd like me to," she added.

"Oh, I'd like you to," he admitted with more eagerness than he had intended to show.

Pleased, Marina smiled back up at him. She wanted to get to know this logger with the straightforward look and that lock of brown hair tumbling down into his eyes.

Jake had focused his thoughts on how he was going to word the invitation. Now that she had accepted, he had no idea what to say next. "I'd better go find Clay," he mumbled and hurried off, leaving a flabbergasted Marina holding the baby.

Eight months ago, Jake had arrived in Manila, his feet hanging off Clay Burrows' logging wagon as if he had nowhere else to go — which he probably didn't.

19

There were so many rumors about him. No one knew where he had come from. Clay, a local landowner, put him to work clearing trees. Jake responded to the opportunity with a passion for hard work and an unshakable loyalty to the man he considered his first friend.

The women in town alternated between being suspicious of a Yankee who had no history he'd admit to and a desire to mother this boy who had no family to speak up for him. The men liked him. Already Jake was developing a reputation as one who would fulfill his part of a bargain and more. He was such a good worker that several of Manila's landowners secretly harbored a regret they hadn't been the one to find him walking down the road.

Just before turning north onto Main Street, Jake looked back to yell, "Ten o'clock two weeks from Saturday, I'll come by your house to get you," then disappeared around the corner.

"Well," Marina addressed her remarks to Oscar. "Judging from his speed, I guess he's a runaway baby like you." She shook her head. "Must have something to do with being a boy."

Chapter Two

November 1912

Marina turned in at the gate designating her grandfather's property. Located at the south end of Main Street, Doc's house was one of the first homes people saw coming into Manila. It was painted bright white. Most homes in Mississippi County weren't painted at all. The house itself was not actually bigger, but wooden pilasters set Doc's home up a little bit higher than the neighbors'.

Although she lived with her mother and brothers on a farm north of town, Marina was a frequent visitor here. Her mother's sixteen-year-old sister was her best friend. Adele waved a good natured greeting and slid over on the porch swing to make room as Marina mounted the steps.

Eddie, Marina's *second* cousin once removed, as she was quick to point out, leaned against the porch. He chomped on a wad of L & M, occasionally sending a hocker flying over the rail.

Doc Bauer sat on the pristine porch, stroking the ends of his handlebar moustache as he reviewed papers spread out on the little table before him. Marina's grandfather had earned the title Doc, not in medical school, but from the sagacity he dispensed on the front porch of his shotgun house. Political cronies and adversaries alike flocked to his platform to hear Doc's solutions to the county's latest troubles. His cronies wanted him to tell them what they were thinking. His enemies wanted the opportunity to disagree.

Immersed in his work, Doc barely looked up as his granddaughter mounted the steps. His attention was fixed on the list of voters in front of him. He was contemplating how each individual would vote, and, if he didn't approve, calculating the probability he could have their ballot disqualified.

Marina settled next to Adele. Reaching for a handful of walnuts from the bowl in her aunt's lap, she shelled nuts while waiting for her grandfather to acknowledge her.

Finally, Doc spoke. Skipping the greeting he considered unnecessary since they both knew she was present, he addressed the topic on his mind. "Marina, I'm countin' on you and Adele to fix the men a nice dinner on Election Day." Doc's demeanor held all the command of a man with influence. "There'll be a lot of people coming by, and I want them feelin' satisfied and agreeable when they leave here to go vote." He delivered the instructions, barely hearing her "yes, sir" before turning back to the voter information.

With a lingering smirk at some private thought, Eddie turned his attention away from the road he'd been watching. "Say, Doc, if the girls fix us an extra nice dinner, how 'bout you let them vote for president?"

Surprised by the suggestion, Marina exchanged a quick look with Adele.

"What's that?" Doc asked, absorbed in his list.

"Don't you think that's a fair trade," Eddie persisted, "A vote for a meal?"

Doc laughed. "Yes, sir. A vote for a meal sounds about right. There are quite a few people here in town I'd like to make that deal with." Doc circled a name on the list and wrote a big question mark in the margin beside it.

Eddie grinned at his cousins. "Just think. You have a chance to do what no other girls in Mississippi County have ever done before. Good thing Doc's so important in town."

Marina tossed the meat of another walnut into the bowl. Why was Eddie being so nice, encouraging Doc to give them a special privilege? Generally, her mother's cousin went out of his way to embarrass or humiliate her with one of his silly jokes. But Doc hadn't seemed surprised by the suggestion. She knew Doc kept track of who voted and who didn't. Walking home from church last Sunday, he'd stopped five different men to say he expected them to vote in this election. Well, if Doc thought she and Adele should vote, then they'd surely do it.

23

Marina spent the night before Election Day at her grandfather's house so she and Adele could be up and working well before dawn. By five-thirty, the yeast bread they had set out the night before was rising nicely. By seven-thirty, sawhorses topped with hickory planks formed makeshift tables on the porch. Adele covered the wood with white cloths, and Marina placed Mason jars filled with homegrown flowers in the center of each table.

For the next three-and-a half-hours, the girls baked, fried, and simmered a feast to rival the abundance of a church potluck. Heaping platters of fried chicken nudged up against bowls brimming with black-eyed peas. Steaming mounds of mashed potatoes surrounded a lake of milk gravy. Marina's eyes surveyed the feast critically, trying to find fault, but failing. Every dish was prepared: a pot of green beans seasoned with bacon grease, a crock of mustard greens dabbed with vinegar, platters of corn on the cob dripping with butter, one tureen filled with summer squash and another with turnips sliced thin, Great-Aunt Diana's spicy-sweet pickles, three jars of jam, and five kinds of pie.

"There's not another thing we can do to make it any better," Adele declared, setting down a pitcher of sweet tea, "and just in time. Here come the first guests."

The men filed up the front steps, brief nods acknowledging the female presence before finding places at one of the tables. After a prayer by Doc, in which he mentioned the political

24

outcome he was expecting the Lord to deliver, the men commenced eating. Marina and Adele stood back, anxiously scanning the men's faces for a hint of anything they might require.

"These biscuits are so light I'm havin' to eat fast to keep 'em from floatin' off my plate," Gene Sikes declared.

"Glad you like 'em," Doc acknowledged. He nodded approval at the girls, who heaved small sighs of relief. Doc was an exacting man, very particular in what he was willing to accept.

The girls would not have needed to fear. The men ate with as much enthusiasm as they politicked, stopping only long enough to call out a good-natured insult or state the same point they'd been pushing for the past eight months. After today, they'd all have to find a new issue to argue over.

Once dinner and the obligatory complaining about having eaten too much were finished, the men reluctantly pulled away from the table. It was time to head down to the polls.

"Don't forget to vote," Eddie reminded Marina as he followed the men. He grinned like a beaver who'd just won first place in a wood chopping contest.

For half a second, Marina considered not voting. She stared after him with the feeling he was playing a joke. She wished this privilege hadn't been Eddie's suggestion. Still, Doc had said it was a good idea. Shaking her head, she dismissed the thought and focused on cleaning up the tables. The girls had a lot of dishwashing to do if they were to vote before the polls closed.

When the last plate had been wiped dry and the trestle tables taken down, they scrubbed their faces and slipped on church clothes. Elegantly, sedately, with a desire to show they understood the gravity of their first vote, Marina and Adele proceeded down the dusty road.

They had almost reached the north end of Main Street where barbed wire separated the business district from cotton fields when Polly Patrice Cox emerged from a store. Dressed in the latest fashion from Blytheville, her former schoolmate stepped onto the wooden sidewalk.

Marina sighed. She had given up trying to like Polly Patrice years ago. It wasn't that Polly Patrice ever said anything outright mean. Even when she flattered, her simpering voice insinuated you were begging for her confirmation.

Determined to be pleasant, Marina faced her old nemesis. This was a historic day for them and no one was going to spoil it. "How are you, Polly Patrice?"

"Wonderful! Marriage is wonderful," the bride of four months answered in a superior tone. "Perhaps one day you'll understand," she added, her tone implying the possibility was doubtful. A frown creased her face. "You seem to be dressed up today. Where are you going?" Polly Patrice did not want to be left out of any social gathering whether she liked the hostess or not.

"We're going to vote," Marina answered, excitement showing in her voice.

26

"Girls can't vote," Polly Patrice dismissed the idea as if Marina were lying.

"We can," Marina asserted. "My grandfather gave us permission."

"Not even Doc Bauer can do that."

For half a second, Marina's courage waned. Could that be true? Was it possible Doc had overstepped his bounds of authority? Then confidence in her grandfather returned. "I guess we'll see," Marina responded matter-of-factly. Stepping around Polly Patrice, the girls crossed Main Street and continued down a side road to the polls.

Marina and Adele paused in front of a two-story wooden building. City Hall with its offices for mayor and town marshal occupied most of the first floor. Steps outside the building led to a second floor which was divided into a jail and a hall where local lodges met regularly. Marina always shuddered when she saw the iron bars on the upstairs windows.

Men milled about the yard. Two civil war veterans played checkers on an old tree stump. They usually competed outside the drugstore but this afternoon had moved across the street so they wouldn't miss the day's excitement.

'Votin' Day' was a cause for celebration in town with many men taking the day off to hang out at the polls even after they had cast their votes. Male voices floated over the light wind, teasing each other, calling out jokes and riddles.

"You know Arkansas is God's favorite place," one man contended.

"I believe it," his buddy agreed.

"I can prove it," the first man asserted.

"Oh, how's that?"

"Well, it's the only place mentioned in the Bible."

"Arkansas's mentioned in the Bible?"

"Yes, sir. Right there in Genesis. It says, 'Noah looked out of the Ark And Saw.'" Both men guffawed.

Several men, Jake Hartmann included, had congregated in front of the entrance to the polls. Talking ceased as the girls approached.

Jake smiled, clearly pleased to see her. Marina paused to identify a few of the other men. Orland Piney was a tall man with a gentle spirit. He attended the Baptist church and was known for his strict honesty in business. Next to him stood Mr. Chapman. Mrs. Chapman bought eggs from their farm each week. Bull Barnes leaned up against the building. Marina avoided looking at him. He was reputed to have a nasty temper with his wife and daughters.

Both girls felt a faint wave of panic sweep over them as they realized Doc wasn't among them. What if he was supposed to have given them a note or a secret password to prove they had permission to vote? Well, then the men could just say so, and they would go get it.

The men stared at Marina and Adele. Behind them, Polly Patrice drew close enough to hear the conversation, curious and, truth be told, not fully convinced that bestowing the power to vote was beyond Doc's ability. The presence of yet a third female at Town Hall on voting day was almost more pressure than the men could bear.

Mr. Piney cleared his throat and tried to move the visit along. "Miss Marina, Miss Adele. That sure was a nice dinner you girls put together for us. We appreciate all your hard work."

"Thank you." Relief flooded over Marina. Clearly, the men understood voting was their reward for the dinner. She waited for instructions on what to do next. When none came, the atmosphere turned awkward again.

Mr. Piney nodded. "Doc's not here. You might find him over at the diner trying to scare up some more votes."

Encouraged by the thought of her grandfather bestowing the privilege of voting on others, Marina replied eagerly. "Oh, we're not here to see Doc."

"You're not?" he asked, clearly puzzled.

"No, sir."

"Well then, what can we do for you?" he asked.

"We're here to vote," Marina explained.

"Vote," several of the men repeated as if they didn't understand the word.

"Yes, sir, for president."

29

At this, the sound of guffawing laughter exploded into the air. Eddie stepped around the corner of Town Hall shaking with hilarity over the success of his prank. His response cued the other men that the incident was a joke. Relieved at no longer having anything required of them, they joined in the laughter. "They came to vote!" Eddie repeated the punch line.

A loud snort escaped Polly Patrice's nose, completely obliterating any pretentions of dignity.

"For president," Eddie added, in case one of the men was missing the point.

Mortified, the girls stood paralyzed, soaking up their shame. Only Jake refused to laugh. "I guess Miss Marina and Miss Adele could vote with more sense than some of you," he commented in a quiet voice. "Seems like I remember hearing a story about somebody around here trying to milk a bull."

The men exploded into laughter. "That was you, Floyd. Not much sense in that."

"I was a kid barely moved here from the city," Floyd protested. "Least it wasn't as bad as the time you came into town braggin' about your huntin' skill. You said you shot the last bear in Mississippi County but claimed he got away in the forest. Turns out, he didn't get far, and he wasn't a bear at all, just that shaggy old cur belongin' to Dover Pikeman."

The men guffawed and tales began to fly with illustrations of how a girl could have more sense than the man standing next to him. Before long they were competing to see who could relate the most entertaining tale.

The girls were forgotten by all but Jake who nodded an encouraging smile at Marina. Seizing the opportunity to escape, the girls turned on polished heels and commenced the humiliating walk past Polly Patrice back up the street to Doc's house.

Chapter Three

November 1912

Aweek passed with Marina successfully avoiding leaving the farm. She hadn't finished one chore before volunteering for another. She milked the cow, churned the butter, scrubbed the farm walls as well as the floors, all the while muttering to herself, "I will never go down to vote again. I don't care how many women finally get the vote. I will never give anyone the chance to humiliate me like that again!"

Finally, her mother's sympathy ran out. "Marina, I'm sorry Eddie played such a mean joke on you, but your life has to go on. You cannot spend the rest of your days in this house regardless of how many chores you're willin' to do. At some point, you're going to have to go to town and you 'bout as well get it over with. Here's a list of groceries I need. Now go!"

Although she practically dragged her feet in the dusty road, the process of putting one foot in front of the other eventually brought even that most reluctant shopper into town. Marina succeeded in purchasing the few items required without seeing Eddie, Polly Patrice, or any of the men from the polls. She especially didn't want to see Jake Hartmann. This coming Saturday was when they were supposed to have gone to the carnival together. That was out of the question now. He probably thought she was the silliest little fool he'd ever met.

She turned toward home. Behind her she could hear the clip clop of an old mule coming into town.

"Marina," a man's voice called out.

Marina cringed. It was him. No doubt he wanted to excuse himself from having to take her to the carnival. Well, she owed him that courtesy. She turned around, determined not to let her disappointment show. Jake had been kind to her. He deserved a pleasant response.

There he sat on top of the mule, smiling as he lifted his hat to her. "Marina, about Saturday. . . ."

Marina nodded, her heart so heavy she didn't trust her voice to words. Here came the excuses.

"It occurred to me," he continued, "that I don't know exactly which farm is yours. Would you mind giving me directions?"

. . .

On Saturday, Marina found herself in a rare disagreement with her mother. "But Mama, I do know him."

33

"Marina, we don't know a thing about his family. Where did you meet him?"

"At church."

"Worship?"

"An ice cream social. It was held at the church."

Hattie ignored the insinuation that any event which took place on church grounds radiated its own holiness. "Marina, he isn't even a Southerner. Where is he from?"

"You can ask him yourself when he comes." The words flew out of Marina's mouth before she had a chance to consider how this reticent young man who never spoke of his past might respond to her mother's personal questions.

Hattie paused. A striking woman with Cherokee ancestry, she possessed high cheekbones and a calm, inscrutable expression. Her square, confident shoulders were adequate for the physical strain of farming and the emotional toil of mothering. Noting the pleading look on her daughter's face, she weighed the possibility of meeting the boy and judging for herself.

"Mama, at least, get to know him. I know you'll like him."

"If he comes, and I don't think he's fit company for you, you'll not say a word when I send him away." It was a decree.

"Oh, Mama, you won't send him away."

"I will if I think he's bad for you." In the almost ten years since her husband's death, Hattie had kept a close eye on her daughter and three sons. Although the house and land were provided by her father, Doc Bauer, she worked the fields like a common farmhand. She and Marina both knew she was capable of disposing with anything she considered a threat to her children. Hattie studied her daughter's face. "If you can accept my decision, then let him come."

.　.　.

Hattie opened the farmhouse screen door. "Why don't you come in and have a seat, Jake. It'll give us a chance to get to know each other." Jake nodded and stepped into the bungalow.

"Where are you from, Jake?"

"Southern Indiana, ma'am."

Marina looked significantly at her mother, as if the bottom half of a Yankee state qualified one for status as a Southerner. Hattie ignored her.

"Any particular town in southern Indiana?"

"Mitchell."

"Do you still have family there?"

He hesitated. "Yes, ma'am. One brother and three sisters."

"Are both of your parents still alive?"

"Yes, ma'am." He looked her squarely in the eye, answering questions politely without offering additional information.

Hattie changed tactics. "How did you meet Clay Burrows?"

"I was lookin' for a job, and he was lookin' for somebody to cut timber. He said he'd give me a try. I've worked for him ever since."

"Eight months?" Hattie wanted to emphasize that he'd been in town less than a year.

"Three years. I've cut logs for Clay from Harrisburg to Manila."

"Three years? How old are you?"

"Eighteen."

"You've been doing a man's work for three years?"

"Yes, ma'am."

Hattie studied his face for a full minute without saying a word. Then, turning to Marina, she announced abruptly, "You may go."

.   .   .

Now that they were alone and strolling along the dirt road toward the fair, Marina felt a sudden shyness come over her. She had been so afraid her mother would not allow her to go that she hadn't allowed herself the luxury of imagining what they might say to each other.

Red oaks on both sides of the lane stretched overhead trying to touch, but the branches still needed a few more years to make it happen. An Indian summer sun shone lazily through the gap, warming their heads and making Marina wish she had not worn this fancy hat with the ribbons that wound around her neck. Looking up, she noticed that the same red and orange trees she had considered so offensive on her walk home from the polls now gleamed like gold in the sun.

For his part, Jake felt comfortable with the silence. He liked the sound of leaves crunching below his feet and the tang of stumps burning in the fields. Occasionally, he took the opportunity to snatch a quick glance at the girl beside him. He wasn't sure which had surprised him more: that she had agreed to go to the fair with him or that he had found the courage to ask.

Marina peeked at Jake from under the brim of her hat. "It's not been easy on Mama — raising my brothers and me by herself," she apologized. "I hope her questions didn't make you feel uncomfortable."

Jake smiled. "If I had a daughter like you, I'd be careful with her too."

"I was afraid she'd be even worse," Marina admitted. "She's probably plannin' to quiz me when we get in tonight."

Jake laughed. "Go ahead and ask me whatever you think she'll want to know."

Marina looked at him questioningly. He nodded encouragement so she continued and asked what *she* wanted to know. "Are you planning to go back to Indiana someday?"

"Never." He responded with vehemence.

"Never?"

"Never. I'll make my home in Arkansas now — probably right here in Manila."

"I'd like that," Marina confessed. "But what about your mother? Won't she be sad?"

"Nope."

"Your daddy?"

Jake gave the question longer consideration before answering. "I'd like to see Daddy again. One day I'll write him a letter and let him know where I am."

"Your brother and sisters?"

Jake looked sad. "I'd like to see them again, but that probably won't ever happen. My parents are divorced." He paused, and Marina tried not to look shocked. "The kids are all spread out. My brother, Jesse, hopped a train before I ever left. Florence was eight the last time I saw her. Mom hired her out as a maid. I don't know what happened to the two little girls. They were pretty small when I left."

"Why did you leave?" Marina asked gently.

"Because I couldn't stay."

"Do you mind talking about your family?"

"Not so much with you. Hey, look! The carnival's just ahead. Have you ever ridden a Ferris wheel before?"

Marina giggled and shook her head. "I'm not sure I want to either. Look how high that goes!"

"You can lean on me when you're afraid," he suggested with a hint of mischief in his eyes.

He bought two tickets and up they went in the swinging basket, their eyes scanning above the tree line. It felt like the world was waiting for them.

When their feet reluctantly touched ground again, Jake announced he was going to have her picture taken. Marina protested, but he cajoled her into it. Afterwards, he was thrilled with the result. She complained the ties on her bonnet made her neck look too long. He insisted she looked beautiful.

They strolled the midway, stopping at every tent that piqued their curiosity. They watched in awe as a glassblower blew into a four-foot pipe, turning the honey-like mixture into a vase. Marina tasted cotton candy for the first time. Jake tried his hand at several arcades including the scarecrow shooting gallery. He not only won a prize for Marina, but one for each of her little brothers as well.

She passed on a chance to see the world's largest snake, and Jake steered her away from the sideshow of harem dancers. They both felt sorry for Tom Thumb and the Giantess but were suspicious the bearded lady was really a man. Marina didn't know it, but Jake spent his savings for a month.

As promised, Jake had her home before dark. He was a smart enough man to know not to mess with Hattie where her daughter was concerned.

Jake became a weekly visitor to the farm, and Hattie allowed him to sit with the family on Saturday evenings. Pleased with her mother's hospitality, Marina never realized the widow's cunning in pulling the young man into their circle where she could get a clear view of his character.

Jake often volunteered to help around the farm. If he saw something that needed doing, he did it without waiting to be asked, an observation not lost on Hattie. She watched, noting Jake's work ethic, the way his words matched his actions, and most of all, the respectful way he treated her daughter.

The days began to get shorter and farmers plowed harvest's leftover cuttings back into the Arkansas soil. Squirrels buried their nuts deep in preparation for cold days and freezing nights. Folks across Mississippi County commented the winter took a bite out of them that year. Marina thought the frost added a shiver of excitement to an already joyful world.

Christmas passed. The sun began to stretch itself and shake off winter. Able to be outside for longer periods of time, the two young people sought privacy by volunteering to run errands for Hattie. They delivered pails of fresh milk to Mrs. Hobert and dozens of eggs to the Chapman house as well as to others in town. Their strolls were filled with gentle teasing, bouts of laughter, and companionable silence. The errands generally took a few minutes longer than Hattie calculated necessary, but not much more.

During one extended saunter they passed a field rampant with wild daisies. Marina smiled. "When we lived out at Big Lake, there was a meadow like this. Every spring it would be covered in daisies. I used to stand in the middle of it and pretend to do ballet. I didn't know exactly what ballet was, but I'd seen a picture of a ballerina in a school book, so I jumped and twirled around the way I thought she might. I imagined all the flowers were the audience watchin' me dance." Embarrassed, Marina ducked her head. She hadn't meant to share that memory. When she was with Jake, who she was just sort of came tumbling out.

"Come dance with me, Marina," Jake invited.

"We don't have any music," she protested to cover her awkwardness.

"I'll sing," he promised.

Marina laughed at his foolishness, but she put her hand in his, allowing him to draw her closer.

A minute later she looked up at him accusingly. "You don't sing. You whistle."

He laughed and pulled her back into the dance. Life was right when they were together.

When dusk signaled the day's end, Jake and Marina settled on the top step of the farmhouse porch. There wasn't much room there and it was a good excuse to sit close. Frank and Wade were finishing up last chores in the barn. Just inside the door, Hattie sat mending Noel's overalls. The little boy drummed on an upturned coffee can, oblivious to the romance not twenty feet away.

"Marina," Jake spoke softly while the crickets and tree frogs sang background music for his proposal. "Bein' with you is

41

like being welcomed home after years of being away. I want to always come home to you. Will you marry me?"

No church ceremony. No friends or relatives. Not even a special wedding dress. Just a wagon ride to Blytheville, seven minutes in the courthouse, then Marina and Jake were married.

And Hattie gave her blessing.

Chapter Four

December 1913

J ake stepped into their sharecroppers' cabin on Clay Burrow's land. Normally, he was content for them to stay out in the woods, but today he felt a little restless. "Let's go to town," Jake urged.

"Now?" Marina asked, pulling the last batch of Christmas cookies out of a wood-burning cook stove.

"Now!" Enthusiasm shone in his eyes. "Today is Christmas Eve. I feel like taking my wife to town."

Marina laughed. "I could give Mama and the boys their Christmas presents. She picked up a hand-stitched handkerchief lying on the kitchen table. "I know Noel would prefer a whistle, but he needs a clean hanky more than he needs a toy."

"Hold on a minute." Jake reached into his pocket and plopped a silver dollar into the middle of the handkerchief.

Marina's eyes widened. "I 'spect Noel will be right pleased with that hanky."

Marina smiled. She loved her husband's generous heart. "I'll clean up my mess here in the kitchen and meet you out front when the wagon's hitched."

Grabbing a basket, she quickly prepared a picnic supper. She cut hunks of roasted chicken from the pot simmering on the stove. Their broth soaked into thick slices of bread as she made sandwiches. A dozen cookies went into the basket, followed by a quart jar of pump water. She could grab a couple of apples from the root cellar on the way out. Not much variety, but feast enough. Covering the basket with a kitchen cloth, she stacked on gifts for her family and a package for the Burrows.

The clop of the mule signaled Jake was ready. Marina threw her coat on, grabbed the basket, and slung a quilt over her shoulder before flying out the door.

Jake stood beside the hitched wagon, grinning as he tossed a couple of apples up in the air and caught them. "I read your mind," he teased, helping her onto the wagon and dropping the apples in her lap. Marina laughed, stuffing the fruit down into the side of the basket where they wouldn't break the cookies.

The wagon rumbled down Right Hand Stumpy Road. Virgin red oak, gum, and walnut trees towered high to the east and west of them. Farmers out at Blackwater and Shady Grove had cleared the old trail leading to town. Jake navigated Ol' Jeb around the tree stumps left in the road.

Marina took a deep breath as they passed a cabin with whiffs of smoke trailing off into the winter sky. She loved the smell of a fireplace burning and cypress wood perfuming the air. The forest had the quiet afternoon stillness of when the day is winding down and the evening critters have not woken up yet.

"I appreciate what Clay's done for me," Jake confided as they rode along. "He gave me a chance and I've pulled my weight. But I don't want to work for somebody else all my life. I want land of my own where I can decide what to plant and where I can set down roots and grow a farm full of children."

Marina squeezed his arm. "I want a home of my own too," she agreed, "one I never have to move from. And," she added shyly, "I want a piano."

Jake looked at her in surprise. She nodded. "Somehow piano music adds to a home's happiness. We had a piano when I was a girl livin' out on the river at Big Lake. I was learnin' to play. Then Papa died, and there wasn't any more money."

Jake put his arm around her pulling her close. "Maybe three more years, Marina. We'll buy us some land and build a house and barn. With land of our own we can get ahead. Then you'll have your piano," he promised.

On Route 18, they stopped by Clay and Thelma Burrows' brick house to deliver the box of cookies and wish the family "Merry Christmas." At the south end of town, Marina presented a package of Christmas cookies to Doc and a smooth blue hair ribbon wrapped in a lace-edged handkerchief to Adele. Back in the wagon, they continued down Main Street, calling out to friends as they passed.

The downtown block boasted groceries, restaurants, a drug store, and hardware retailers. Oil and gas lamps lit the stores, throwing a romantic holiday feel over the late afternoon. Shop doors were flung open to accommodate townspeople and farmers making rounds from one business to the next. Shouts of holiday greetings seasoned the air.

Jake drove past the school and cemetery to the north end of town. No more holiday cheer could be heard. People commotion gave way to the sounds of farmland edging up against the forest of Big Lake. When the road had gone as far north as the timberland would allow, Jake turned the mule east, silently smiling as he remembered walking Marina down this road while they were courting. A few minutes later the wagon pulled to a stop between the barn and the farmhouse.

"Marina and Jake are here!" Her brothers were out in the yard yelling before they could dismount.

Hattie noticed how carefully Jake helped Marina down out of the wagon. Her smile grew even bigger. She held Marina's arm, looked her in the eye, and joyously asked, "When is my first grandbaby due?"

Marina laughed. "I never could hide anything from you, Mama. The baby's comin' in May."

The family trooped inside the little farmhouse. Hattie poured Jake and Marina each a mug of coffee. "I'm so glad you came by," she beamed. And then, as if her joy needed a way to work out of her body, she grabbed up a slotted spoon and resumed frying half-moon peach pies in a black iron skillet. The aroma of spiced peaches filled the kitchen.

Marina grinned as she pulled an orange out of her pocket. Knowing the sweet smell would drive her brothers crazy, she peeled it quickly, dividing the sections into three. Each of her brothers stuck as large a section as possible into his mouth, competing to see who could suck the juice out first.

They exchanged family news while Hattie transferred the half-moon pies to a cloth-covered platter so they could drain off the grease. Within minutes they were all exclaiming over the touch of cinnamon in the sweet dessert.

Finally, Marina could stand the wait no longer. She handed her eldest brother a thin package wrapped in brown paper. "This is for you, Frank."

"A knife!" he yelled, tearing his present open. "I knew it! It's a knife!" He hugged his sister, then promptly slipped out the door, looking for a good piece of wood to whittle.

"Wade!" Her middle brother didn't wait to be called twice. It was obviously a book and he tore the brown wrapping off with glee.

"*Robinson Crusoe*," he hollered. His sister received a rushed half-hug before he raced from the room to begin reading.

Marina watched him run, then turned back to the table to find little Noel standing next to her, not speaking a word, but eyes begging not be forgotten.

"We have something very special for you, Noel," Marina promised. His eyes lit up, but still he said nothing. "Jake has it in his pocket."

Nine-year-old Noel turned to face his brother-in-law. Jake smiled as he pulled the white handkerchief out of his pocket. He placed it in Noel's cupped hands.

The little boy felt the weight inside the cloth before carefully unwrapping it. When he reached the center and saw the silver dollar, his eyes opened as wide as the coin.

"This is your very own silver dollar, Noel" Jake explained. "Whenever you get a silver dollar, you need to hold onto it tight. Do you promise?"

Noel looked up from the dollar into Jake's eyes. "I promise," he committed solemnly before retreating to his seat, where he used the handkerchief Marina had painstakingly hemmed to shine his treasure.

Next Marina placed a large box on the table. Hattie exclaimed with pleasure as she lifted out the Christmas coconut cake her daughter had baked that morning. No girl ever outgrows the need for her mother's approval. Marina beamed with pleasure as her mother praised her.

"I didn't have any paper for wrappin', but this is for you." Hattie placed her pink glass butter dish with domed lid on the table. Marina looked at her mother in surprise. "You always liked it even as a kid," Hattie declared. "You should have it."

"Thank you, Mama." Marina leaned over and kissed her.

Jake took another sip of coffee and unfolded the freshly pressed shirt Hattie laid in front of him. The shirt had belonged to Marina's father, a costly gift indeed since it could have been remade to fit sons she was still providing for.

"Thank you, ma'am."

They chatted for a little bit longer, then Marina kissed her mother and the boys goodbye. She felt satisfied. The sun eased into a lazy descent and the temperature followed as the wagon retraced its route to town.

Jake hitched his wagon to a metal post in front of a large one-story brick store. They stepped down onto planks serving as a make-shift sidewalk and joined the parade of shoppers. Some of the townspeople were throwing caution and budget to the wind in a burst of celebratory spirit. Others, like themselves, were content with soaking up the atmosphere. They could hear farmers and townspeople cheering as the train tooted its arrival at the depot. The town's last holiday guests had arrived.

For almost an hour, Jake and Marina walked up one side of Main Street and down the other. Every child on the street seemed to have a peppermint stick in hand. Like all parents-to-be since Adam and Eve, they wondered what their own child would look like. They paused outside the bakery and ogled the tempting display of sweets in the window.

"Yours are better," Jake whispered, pulling out a couple of Marina's sugar cookies to nibble on.

"You haven't tasted the bakery's," Marina whispered back.

"Don't need to." Her husband settled the issue.

A trio of friends attempted to serenade fellow shoppers with carols. Laughter and missed lyrics prevented them from completing a song, so the result was more merry than melodious.

Evening had fallen and they knew they had better head back. The bright lights of town would not reach as far as Right Hand Stumpy Road. Jake fed Ol' Jeb what was left of their apples and guided the wagon south toward home.

Forests on both sides of the road muffled the sounds of others sharing their world. A light snow began to fall—fun anytime—but on Christmas Eve, clearly a show of favoritism from God.

Marina soaked it all in—the beauty of the night, the physical closeness of her husband, their baby held within, and the thrill of a future filled with possibilities. She took a deep breath, inhaling the moment as well as the air. "Would you know what I meant if I said this is a crystal moment?" Marina asked softly. "Right now, in this bit of time, the world is perfect. It almost feels as if it isn't real. There's only beauty. The perfection seems so pure, it physically hurts. It's fragile. The slightest disturbance could shatter it into a thousand pieces. It almost makes me feel afraid."

"Don't be afraid, Marina." Jake switched the reins to his left hand and wrapped his arm around her. "I guess life will hold enough surprises for us down the road. Maybe everything won't be exactly like we're picturin'. But this joy is real. Tonight, we'll take the joy."

Chapter Five

February 1914

February's pale sun rays touched the back of Marina's neck. Inching her way along the path, she smoothed dirt over her seeds, carefully tapping down any air pockets. With a small grunt to accommodate the baby due to make an appearance in three months, she stood up, assessing her first garden as Mrs. Jacob Hartmann.

The rows of soil were neatly formed. She had enough room for weeding, but no wasted space. Her eyes followed the garden path, seeing lettuce, tomatoes, carrots, peppers, beans, peas, and cabbage yet to be. She could grow almost all the food her family needed.

Marina tilted her head to the side, estimating the produce her share of Eden would yield. It was possible she had gotten a little carried away on the size of her garden. She was used to planting with her mother and three brothers in mind. No matter. She'd be proud to share.

Out of the corner of her eye Marina was distracted by a fuzzy-looking stem. Two steps brought her within reach of the culprit. She bent down and yanked up the offending shoot. "That's better," she muttered.

Satisfied with the morning's work, Marina picked up the box of seeds her mother had given her and started back to the house. Her eyes lit on the sharecroppers' cabin in the middle of cleared land, and her face took on a critical expression.

The bungalow sat on nine cement foundation blocks. Chinking in between the logs was good and tight. Jake had made sure of that before winter set in. The porch rested level on boulders brought in from the field. For a tenant's cabin it looked alright. It had two rooms, plenty of space for such a small family. Still, something was missing. It looked colorless. . ., impersonal, as if it could belong to any sharecropping family in Mississippi County.

She didn't feel that way about the inside of their home. Jake had built all their furniture. She and her mother had sewn every stitch of curtain, kitchen towel, and dishrag Marina and Jake owned. Their bedcover boasted bright cheerful colors. There was something so intimate about a quilt made up of little bits and pieces of your past. Every detail in the cabin divulged something about who they were. Each object had a space where it belonged. The glass butter dish Mama had given her for

Christmas held place of honor on the shelf. It was never used because she didn't want to risk breaking it, but it belonged.

Outside the cabin, however. . . .Marina studied the clearing. It was tidy. . ., organized. . .*dirt*, swept dirt even, with an occasional tree stump waiting to be burned out. Only two small bushes grew within dish-water-throwing distance of the house.

She understood the need to clear land, but. . . .Marina's mind shifted to the house where her mother lived. The old farmhouse was surrounded by a grassy yard dotted with old oak trees and a wild dogwood that had sprung up close to the pump. A grove of black walnut trees separated the yard from the cotton fields. It was a busy place, but pleasant.

Before moving to the farm near town, they had lived at Big Lake. Marina's mind turned to her first home. Nothing could be more different from a dry sharecropper's clearing than Big Lake. It was labeled *The Great Swamp* on school maps. A forest of river birch, sycamore, cottonwoods, ash, hickory, and hackberry trees surrounded open waters and bottomland marsh. The forest held shades of green so intense, so wild you could close your eyes and still feel the beauty soaking into your skin. Marina smiled at the memory of huge bald cypress trees sticking up out of the lake and tupelos reflecting the water so perfectly it was hard to tell where sight of the trunk ended and mirror image of bark began.

After the War Between the States, pioneers had pushed west, leaving northeast Arkansas one of the few unexplored wildernesses in America. Except for the cluster of cabins near the steamboat dock and Dunkin Ice House at Timm's Point, a person could go several miles through the forest before seeing another home. She never remembered feeling lonely, though.

As a child, she had named individual trees and assigned personalities. The weeping black willow up on the rise was Mrs. Drip. Poor old thing, she'd cry just as soon as look at you. Mrs. Hickory, on the other hand, was stern and proper. Then there were the Buttonbush boys. In her imagination they created as much mischief as her brothers.

What a rich start to life Big Lake had given her. She wanted that for her own children. Marina looked at the dirt again. Well, the dirt was rich delta soil anyway and all this cleared land would provide plants with plenty of sun. Hollyhocks could grow at least ten feet tall, maybe higher. Good thing too. Their flaming blooms would encourage a person to look beyond the lack of grass. She eyed the bushes. Leaves could help cover the gap between earth and where the floor of the house sat on foundation blocks. Maybe she could find some purple maypops nearby to transplant before the next acreage was cleared. Marina grinned. Jake would love hearing maypops were known as *passion flowers*.

She sighed, remembering the wild roses her mother had cultivated near the old cabin stoop. Too bad she couldn't go out to Big Lake and dig up what she needed. Sure would brighten this place up.

She paused. Well, why not? The swamp nurtured a gorgeous array of wildflowers: dark blue larkspur, purple cone flowers, white shooting stars, and silly sunflowers that popped up wherever they had a mind to.

Suddenly Marina felt an aching to go back out to Big Lake. She wanted to smell the earthiness of damp ground, to feel the moisture in the air, to see thousands of ducks crowding each other's space on the water. She wanted Jake to see it too.

Footsteps sounded behind her as Jake walked up. "Garden looks real good," he complimented.

"Hmm, the garden? Oh, yes. I'm satisfied with the vegetable plot, but not the yard. We need flowers to bring some color to the place." Mind made up, she turned to convince him. "Jake, I'd like to go back home to dig up starts for plantin' around our cabin."

Jake looked at her in surprise, then glanced at the tiny bushes on each side of the stoop. "The plantings your mother gave you seem to be doin' alright."

"I mean back home to Big Lake, to the cabin where we lived until Papa died. The swamp grows every color of flower under the sun, flowers you can't find anywhere else. I want to transplant them here where our children will grow up."

"Marina, we're going to live in this house only two or three more years. When I've finished clearin' this forty acres, Clay will want us to move closer to the next forty. Wouldn't you rather wait to do all that work until after we have a home of our own?"

56

"I'd rather make this a home of our own now. When we move to a new cabin, I'll dig up my plants and move them too."

"Big Lake's a good three miles east of Manila. Are you sure you even feel up to spending all that time bouncin' around in the wagon?"

Marina patted her stomach gently. "I'm fine. In fact, I have more energy than I usually do."

Jake sighed. He thought it was a waste of time, but Marina didn't ask for much, and frankly, nine months of marriage had taught him his wife could be a little more stubborn than he had originally suspected. "Well, I suppose if you change your mind, you could leave the plants here for the next family. Alright, we'll go on Saturday."

A shovel, tin bucket, and burlap wrap were stashed in back, ready for digging. The closer they got to Big Lake, the more Marina leaned forward in the wagon. She barely paid attention as they passed through town. Her heart and mind were already in the forest.

"How long after your father died did you move close to town?" Jake asked as they plodded along.

"One week. Doc sent a wagon and two men out to the cabin. Mama hadn't even known they were comin'. They rolled the wagon up to the clearing, knocked on the door, and said, 'Doc says to bring you back. What do you want in the wagon?'"

"I thought Mama would argue with them, tell them no. I couldn't imagine livin' anywhere else. It was the only home the boys and I had ever known. Mama always understood how I felt, but that time she never even looked at me. She stared out the window for a minute, glanced down at her belly — she was seven months pregnant with Noel — and said, 'We'll need the beds, the rocker, the table, and chairs. It won't take me long to pack the dishes and the clothes.'

"And it hadn't. In less than an hour everything we were taking with us was packed on that wagon. We didn't even leave dirt. Mama swept the place clean."

Marina lapsed into silence, memories taking her back over the years. They rode along for a while before Jake commented. "I've heard some of the men refer to Big Lake as a river. Which is it?"

"Accordin' to our old Manila schoolmaster, who is also Doc's brother and my Great-Uncle Benjamin, it was part of the Mississippi River system until the big earthquake a hundred years ago. That earthquake sank this whole area and created the lake. Uncle Benjamin claims the quake was ten times as powerful as the one they had in San Francisco in '06." She grinned. "Of course, he wasn't actually there in 1811. He's guessin', but his guesses are usually pretty good."

Jake nodded. "I've heard the area's great for huntin' and fishin'."

"You can hunt anything there. Papa was a market duck hunter, but he also brought home wild turkey, fish, turtles, swamp rabbit, raccoon, 'possums — everything you can find

58

in the woods for our family. He gave away a lot of meat too. Just ahead there—curve to the left and it'll bring us close to the water at Timm's Point."

Eager to catch a glimpse of the swamp, Marina leaned so far forward Jake feared she might take a nosedive over the front. He kept one eye on Ol' Jeb and an eye and a hand ready to pull his wife back by the skirt if necessary. They rounded the path and the forest pushed back to reveal Mississippi County's swamp community.

Chapter Six

February 1914

arina jumped down from the wagon without waiting to be helped. Within seconds she covered a short incline leading to the edge of the great swamp. There in the cypress-dotted water, mallards crowded so thick she could see only speckles of light hitting water beneath them. Delighted, Marina stood still, paying tribute to what felt like a sacred moment.

Jake followed her, glancing around in surprise at the amount of activity within the clearing. Half a dozen children played between two log cabins while a woman hung out laundry next to a third cabin. Two women chatted at the pump, and a man entered what appeared to be a scaled-down general store. Concrete steps led from the edge of the water up to a long wooden building he couldn't identify. He noticed a couple of houseboats tied up at the landing. "I didn't realize there would be this much goin' on," Jake commented. "I thought Big Lake would be backwoods."

Marina looked sideways at him. "This is backwoods."

"But there are cabins and people. I thought it would be nothin' but trees and swamp water. People claim the Great Swamp is uninhabitable."

"Most of it is," Marina admitted. "You can go north or south for miles and run into only hunters, a trapper, or maybe an old Indian. Not too many of those left."

"How far do the woods and the swamp stretch?"

"About a hundred miles. They go north into Missouri too."

Jake shook his head, trying to take it all in. "Weren't you afraid of livin' out here when you were a little girl?"

"Afraid of what?"

He shrugged. "Panthers, bears, livin' in the wilderness instead of town."

Marina shook her head. "Big Lake was all I knew. Our family rarely went to town. Panthers were out at night, but that was long after I was tucked in bed."

She looked across the lake, letting the tranquility of the waters sink into her. "I don't think anybody has seen a bear out here for a long while. When I was a little girl, Papa hunted bear. He didn't go out specifically lookin' for 'em, but if one came a little too close, he'd bring it on home. That was a treat! Mama made the best bear sausage you ever tasted, and Papa hung the fur up on the east wall of the cabin to keep the wind from whistlin' in. Back then, my brothers were so little our family couldn't eat a whole bear before it spoiled." She laughed. "Sure would be different now. I 'spect Mama'd be proud to have a couple hundred pounds of meat to roast, and the boys sure would be proud to eat it. She kept the bear's bladder in case one of us got fever. Papa traded the oil for flour and other supplies. And, too, we always shared the feast with neighbors. It wouldn't do to keep somethin' that good all to yourself."

"Look at those two ducks over there," Jake pointed. Two ducks were staging a polite quarrel and nudging each other for more space on the water. Marina laughed out loud.

"Some of the local men in town were talkin' 'bout the real duck wars. They said it'd been goin' on for about forty years. How did the duck wars get started? Did you know about them when you were a little girl?"

"Oh, I knew, alright. We all did. I remember scrunchin' down under the quilts at night, listenin' to Mama and Papa whisper. Big city businessmen often came for sport huntin'. That was alright with everybody. Some of the men even made a little extra money as guides. But then the sports, that's what we called 'em, built their clubhouse and got greedy. They claimed market hunters like my Papa would shoot all the ducks and there wouldn't be any left for them to hunt with their buddies. They bought a strip of land on each side of the lake and demanded market hunters stop shootin' on the swamp. Of course, the local men ignored them and kept right on huntin'.

The sports had big money and a line of friends all the way to Washington. The federal government sided with the sports. Can you believe that?"

Jake shook his head.

"Papa was normally a quiet, easy-going man, but when that happened, he banged the table with his fist and said, 'How can some fool in Washington tell me I cain't hunt ducks in the same waters I've been huntin' since I was seven years old? My pappy hunted ducks right here and my grandpappy before that. They want me to give up feedin' my family so some city boys can spend a week or two in the country and pretend they own it?' I never saw Papa so mad!"

"Were you worried the government would force your family off of Big Lake?"

"No. Papa said he wouldn't let it happen and I believed him. The local hunters kept right on huntin'. The sports tried to have it enforced, but the sheriff and the county judges were smart enough to know if they didn't turn a blind eye, come the next election, they'd be out of a job."

"What did the huntin' club do?"

"They hired armed guards."

"What did the local market hunters do?"

"They shot right back at 'em. Then, somehow, the clubhouse burned down so the sports didn't have anywhere to stay."

"It's so beautiful out here, so peaceful, it's hard to believe there could be so much violence. Even aside from the duck wars, I've heard stories about wild goin's-on at the huntin' lodge," Jake commented.

"I 'spect they're true, although I can't personally verify it. The lodge was a ways south of here." She laughed somewhat ruefully. "That lodge was the cause of the only spankin' Papa ever gave me."

Jake raised his eyebrows and waited for an explanation.

A bit sorry she had admitted to anything, Marina felt compelled to continue. "I was eight or nine. I had always heard stories of what went on in there when the big sportsmen came down from Chicago—nothin' specific, of course, just bits of adult conversations that were hushed up whenever children came into the room. Papa made it a point to tell me, 'Don't you go near that huntin' lodge.' It was a good distance away, so there really wasn't any danger I'd get there, but I still asked why. He said, 'Marina, I told you not to go. Now that's the end of it.'

"I rarely disobeyed him. Even as a child I understood the dangers of livin' at the swamp. At nine, I could probably identify animal tracks better than some of the sports. But, here was the outside world coming into my territory and I had to stay away. It bothered me somethin' fierce. I thought city folks were stranger than animals, and I wanted to get a good look at 'em.

"Then one day Mama sent me over to the store, and I met a girl from Buck's Point. Buck's Point's on the other side of Big

Lake. That girl bragged about how she got to go to the huntin' club ever' night. Probably wasn't true, but I believed it at the time. Made me so mad I told her I was goin' that very night and I'd see her there."

"Did you?" Jake asked, captivated by this rebellious side of his gentle wife.

"I tried. I waited until after dark and sneaked off but didn't get very far down the road. I heard a bobcat caterwaul and high-tailed it right back home. Papa was already comin' after me. I promised I didn't see anything, but he spanked me anyway. He said I might get braver as I got older, and he wanted to give me somethin' strong enough to remind me sneakin' off to the huntin' club was a bad idea. It worked. Here I am married with a baby comin' and I still remember."

Not wanting to continue the discussion, Marina switched subjects. "There's the Dunkin Ice House." She pointed to the long wooden building beside the water. The door opened and a duck hunter strolled out, his feet tracking sawdust used to insulate the ice. "Duck hunters store the birds at Dunkin's until they can get 'em to market. I always loved it when Big Lake froze. Frank and I would come down to watch the men saw ice into blocks."

A thin man strode past them on his way to a homemade houseboat. Marina glanced at him and her face broke out in a wide smile. "Mr. Beckhart?"

The hunter turned to see who was calling him. A look of astonishment appeared across his face as he switched directions, hurrying toward them. "Little Marina! I haven't seen you since we lost your pa to pneumonia. How are you, honey? You're as pretty as ever." He looked at Jake, prompting an introduction.

"Pleased to meet you." The two men exchanged greetings and shook hands.

"You from around here?" Mr. Beckhart asked.

"No, sir. Not originally. I was born in Indiana." Jake paused, always reticent to share personal information. James Beckhart waited patiently for more details so Jake added, "We lived all over Vigo, Owen, and Lawrence counties."

"Thought I recognized your Hoosier accent. My family's from Warsaw, Indiana, up towards the top half of the state. Ever been that far north?"

"No sir. Can't say as I have."

"Good land up there, some of it swamp, but nothin' that beats the huntin' 'round Big Lake. I followed the mallards on down. Started out livin' in a tent, but then the missus and me built us a houseboat. We settled over at Buck's Point."

"Are you still guidin' sports through the swamp?" Marina asked.

"Nah, I've kinda slowed down the last few years, spend most of my days carvin' duck calls."

"Mr. Beckhart's duck calls are famous," Marina explained to Jake.

"They do alright," Mr. Beckhart agreed. "'Course the hunters don't really need 'em. Mallards 'round here are so thick a couple dozen fall out of the sky ever' time a gun fires."

Jake's eyes scanned from one end of the bird-covered marsh to the other. "I've never seen anything like it. There must be a couple hundred thousand ducks on the lake right now."

Marina laughed. "Papa always said he never had to hunt a duck. He claimed he'd just take the boat out on the lake of a morning, wake the mallards up, and say, 'Come on now. You best go with me.' And they'd dive right into the boat all by themselves."

James Beckhart nodded. "That's about the truth of it. Fortunately, those city sports from St. Louis, Chicago, and Memphis like takin' my calls home as a memento of their adventure into the swamp."

"They buy them even though they don't need them?" Marina asked, curious.

"Yep. Two-fifty for the plain ones. Five dollars if they're hand-checkered or I carve a turtle or a gun on it."

"Well," she answered practically, "they're gettin' a good duck call whether they use it down here or not."

"Yep. Way I figure it, they're all set to attract the local ducks when they git back home."

"That's if a sport can figure out which end of the gun to fire," Marina added.

A delighted smile spread over the veteran hunter's face. "I believe I see a bit of your pa in you."

Marina laughed. "I suppose you do."

"When is huntin' season?" Jake asked.

Mr. Beckhart surveyed the ducks crowding the lake. "Here in Mississippi County we say it's from the time the ducks fly in until the time the ducks fly out. Well, I'd better be getting' on home for dinner. Jake, good to meet you. If you ever get back up to the home state, say hello to it for me." He paused, "You've got yourself a good girl there. You take care of her. Marina, you tell Miz Hattie hello for me, will you?"

"I sure will and please give my best to Mrs. Beckhart."

"Will do. She'll be pleased to hear you're doin' so well."

"Nice meetin' you, Mr. Beckhart." They watched him step into his handmade boat. As if out of respect for a man that could speak their language, the mallards parted for his boat. His oar hit the water with a practiced stroke as he wound his way among the cypress and tupelos and was lost from sight.

The lure of the swamp drew Marina's eyes to the tree-studded water. The air felt lighter here, easier to breathe, perhaps because of so many trees. "I still can't imagine anything more beautiful. Come summer, there's a swimmin' spot here that's clear as fresh rainwater."

"We better get movin' too if we're goin' to dig up those plants we came after," Jake commented.

Marina turned to face the cluster of buildings. "We lived west of those houses, farther back in the woods." They walked back up the incline, stopping beside Ol' Jeb to collect empty buckets, tools, and odds and ends of burlap scraps. Marina led the way behind the cluster of cabins and down a footpath that had all but disappeared. They walked for a few minutes before a series of squawks caused Marina to freeze in place. She listened for a moment, a look of rapture on her face, then pointed north into the holly bush. A rafter of turkeys strutted out in formation. "Bawk, bawk, bawk, bawk. Bawk." The wild birds crossed the path fifteen yards ahead of them, acknowledging the intruders' existence with a disapproving, beady eye. Marina grinned. Years slipped away and she was once again a little girl winding her way home.

The farther into the woods they tramped, the more the birds ignored them, chirping loudly and carrying on their business as if the young couple were no more than trees crashing in the forest.

"Watch your step," Jake cautioned as they reached a gushing stream.

Marina laughed, stepping lightly over the slippery rocks to arrive at the other side of the stream. She paused, studying a beaver's dam and lodge while she waited for her husband. "Turn to the left just past that big old birch. It was my favorite tree," she added.

69

"In the middle of the forest you had a favorite tree?" Jake asked, incredulous.

"I certainly did."

At a loss for how to respond, he asked, "What did you like about this one?"

"Its personality. It's much friendlier than any other tree in the forest," she asserted, patting its trunk as they passed.

Jake stared at the bark curling back in beautiful spirals. He couldn't see a difference between it and any other birch trees. He decided not to share that opinion with his wife.

Marina read his expression and laughed. "Indiana's full of forests. Weren't you friends with your trees?"

"I was more interested in the caves. My brother, Jesse, and me spent every moment we could get away, crawlin' through caves around Mitchell, Indiana. We thought we were the first to discover them."

"Through here," she instructed. They stepped out of the woods and into a clearing about a fourth of an acre long. In the center stood an unhewn oak cabin almost camouflaged by the untouched forest.

Marina stood still with a puzzled expression on her face.

"What's the matter?" Jake asked gently.

"It's just that. . .it looks so small. I remember our cabin as being much larger."

"It probably did seem a lot larger to you at that time. You're not such a big woman. I don't suppose there was much of you as a girl."

Marina stood silent, trying to come to terms with the difference between her memory of eleven years and the facts she had known for thirty seconds. She shook her head. The memory seemed more real.

They walked toward the old cabin, and Marina nodded to the front porch, catching the last of the morning rays. "Mama used to call that the preacher's porch 'cause it's where the travelin' preacher would stay when he came through. Once we moved to town, we switched to callin' it the front porch like Doc does."

Jake grinned. "No preacher's porch for Doc?"

"Doc never met a preacher whose politics he agreed with enough to let the man sleep on his porch."

Although clearly deserted, evidence of loving care still clung to the place. Weeds had won the war with Hattie's former flower patch. Remnants of what had once been carefully tended flower beds had begun their spring push through the soil. Stubborn native plants refused to give in, and an occasional sprout could be seen lifting its head above the more common spikes.

Suddenly the memories and grief of losing her father overwhelmed Marina. She didn't want to go into the cabin again. Instead, she dropped to her knees. Pulling the hand spade out of a worn burlap sack, she began digging out the roots of her childhood.

She searched for slips of greenery that had the stamina to be transplanted every three or four years. As she worked, Marina pondered early memories, eliciting incidents she hadn't thought about in years. She remembered her father and his beautiful dark eyes that drooped at the corners. She smiled, remembering how his whole face would light up when she met his boat coming in at the landing.

Every hundred yards or so, she'd stop to examine a leaf on a plant or vine. Not many flowers were blooming, so she paid attention to how the leaves were attached to the stalk and compared their sizes with others nearby. She rejected some plants for weak roots and scrutinized others for spots and changes in color.

Jake stood by, ready to dig where instructed. Some shrubs she stuck in a pail of water; others she wrapped in burlap scraps. Occasionally, she'd take the trowel herself, using the steel end to mark a wide circle around the parameter. Then she pushed the shovel straight down into the soil, gently wiggling the tool, allowing the plant to free itself from the earth.

"Don't you trust me with your most valuable plants?" Jake teased.

"Well, you do spend most of your days choppin' down trees," she reminded him.

Marina's treasure hunt lasted over four hours. Finally, she was satisfied she had enough plants to surround her home with flowers.

Delighted, Marina spent the drive home visualizing exactly where each plant would go. She glanced up as the wagon turned in beside their cabin. Although it was still light, a third-quarter moon could be seen rising through the trees. She nodded to herself. This was a good night to plant.

Eager to turn her ideas into reality, Marina was digging before Jake had put the mule and the wagon up for the night. Without talking except to occasionally ask him to hand her a plant or a tool, she focused on digging and planting. The last seeding brought great satisfaction and the realization she was exhausted. Marina used the handle of the shovel to steady herself as she stood. Every root had been planted. The yard didn't look as full and rich as it would in summer when the flowers would bloom and the leaves had time to spread out, but it certainly looked as if someone lived here. No more tenants' dirt clearing. Her family would have a yard.

Just one more thing to do. Reaching down to an early bloom on the primrose, she snapped off its only bud and headed into the house. To Jake's surprise, instead of putting the bloom into a jar, she tossed its flower onto a pile of dried flowers resting in a cracked, painted wash bowl.

"Isn't that the bowl you keep for drying flower seeds?" Jake asked, curious.

"No. This is my potpourri and I'm adding the first bloom from our family flower garden."

"It's your what?"

"Potpourri. Ever since I was a little girl, I've kept a dish of dried flowers. Each bloom represents something from my life. Some sad, like the wild yellow roses planted near Papa's grave, but most of them happy memories. Do you remember bringing me flowers when we were courtin'? They're all in here. Mixed together, these blooms make up my life." She laughed at the confused look on her husband's face. "Come on. I'll boil you a cup of coffee before we go to bed."

Chapter Seven

May 1914

"Jake," Marina's voice shook with pain. "Wake up, I need you."

Jake bolted upright out of a dead sleep. This was the moment. He slipped on his pants while his mind struggled to focus. "Are you alright? What do you need?" He lit the kerosene lamp on the dresser so that he could see her face.

"I need Dr. Franklin," she whispered.

Jake punched his arms through the shirt sleeves, stuffing sockless feet into work boots. Thinking through his plan of action, he stopped, turned back around toward his wife, and gave the useless command always given to women in labor. "Don't do *anything* until I get back!"

Another contraction hit and Marina balled handfuls of the quilt in both fists. Out of breath from the pain, she nodded that she had heard him.

Satisfied that as the man, he now had the situation under control, he disappeared into the night. In less than three minutes, she heard the sound of Ol' Jeb thundering down the road a little faster than most mules think they can go.

They were back within an hour.

After Dr. Franklin disappeared behind the bedroom curtain, Jake wandered around the house, waiting. He kept listening for a baby's cry, but didn't hear anything other than muffled words between Marina and the doctor. Now that he and the doctor were back, why didn't Marina just go ahead and have the baby?

Jake looked for something to do. He *needed* something to do. Unfortunately, Marina never went to bed with a dish unwashed. He tried straightening the already-straight dishrag looped over the dishpan but only made it crooked. Finally, he gave up housekeeping, lit a kerosene lantern, and went outside to chop wood by lamp light.

Eventually a circle of orange haze announced an end to the long night. Jake had split enough kindling to last them through next winter when he heard a little cat cry. Surprised, he checked behind the wood pile—nothing there.

"Jake," Dr. Franklin's voice called from the door. "Come meet your new daughter."

He made it through the house in three strides. Entering the bedroom, Jake anxiously searched Marina's face for signs of distress. She was worn out, but there was a look of utter contentment on her face.

"Look at her!" Marina motioned to the bundle that lay on her arm. Wrapped in a baby quilt, the tiniest person he had ever seen captured his heart. About five pounds of sugar, she appeared more fragile than he remembered from the births of his sisters. Her big blue eyes looked out of a round face with flushed pink cheeks. Fluffs of light brown hair were matted down, still wet from the cleaning the doctor had given her.

Jake stared, almost unable to move.

"Would you like to hold her?" Marina prompted.

That moved him to action. He backed away. "No, no. I mean I would, but she's so tiny. I better wait until she's bigger. Probably by the time she's three or four, I could hold her."

Marina shook her head at his nonsense. "Come here and hold your daughter," she commanded gently.

Jake looked to the physician who nodded permission. "But it wouldn't hurt for you to sit down," Dr. Franklin added.

Jake settled onto the feather bed beside his wife and daughter, cautiously, still reluctantly, taking possession of this little girl who now owned him.

"Well, my work here is done," Dr. Franklin smiled, snapping his black bag shut. "Send for me if you need to, but I 'spect you'll be fine." He showed himself out, leaving the two new parents staring at this precious gift that he predicted would give them much love and a fair share of worry.

Eventually, Jake handed his daughter back to the one he trusted most. Without a word he slipped down the bungalow's front steps to the wild rose bush Marina had transplanted from the swamp. Snapping his pocket knife open, he sliced off two perfect pink roses, one in full bloom, the other a tightly closed rosebud. Both still had drops of morning dew on them.

Returning to his family, he handed the open flower to his wife, then caressed the baby's cheek with the bud. Instinctively, she turned her tiny mouth toward the feel of the petals.

Her parents laughed, totally amazed that she even existed. "Let's name her 'Rosa Lee,'" Marina suggested.

Jake nodded. He glanced down at the rose bud still in his hand and tossed it into the potpourri.

. . .

Marina peeked in on seven-month-old Rosa Lee lying peacefully in the middle of their feather bed. She sighed contentedly. Winter evenings like this were the best.

Everything was so peaceful. It was hard to believe all of Europe had been fighting since last year. The papers were full of news about it. Thank goodness the war didn't have anything to do with the United States — although some people were saying they thought America should get involved.

She walked past Jake reading the paper and to the dresser in the living room. Smiling, she opened the second drawer and almost reverently took out the thick book. This was the moment she had been waiting for all day. Pulling close to the wood stove, Marina let out a sigh of delight as she opened the Sears & Roebuck catalogue.

She had her system for studying the catalogue down to an art. Straightaway, she went to the latest in sewing machines. Wouldn't that be somethin' to have a machine to do the stitchin' for you! Marina guessed she'd be able to sew a dress before supper.

She skipped to housewares. It was really hard to believe any kitchen could use that many pots and pans. What else did you need but an iron skillet and a good-sized pot?

Jake turned the page of the *Arkansas Sentinel* he was reading. "Can you believe more people in the United States live in the city than do in the country now?" he asked.

Marina stopped leafing through the catalogue and turned to look at him. "Why?" she asked.

"I have no idea."

Marina shook her head and turned to the clothes section. She flipped through men's fashions for a few minutes before a ridiculous sight caught her eye. She sat there stunned. Who would have thought! Right there it advertised *Invisible Trouser Support* promising to "hold a man's trousers up and his shirt down."

"My goodness, what would Jake do if I ordered him one of those?" she mused. A few pages later she paused to wonder over a collection of detachable rubber collars. She shook her head. "That'd burn his neck up out in the cotton field."

Next, she skipped to the section on vegetables. Marina had plenty of seeds from this past summer to start the garden in a couple of months. What she really would love to do was order a new flower seed, maybe a zinnia. Or perhaps she should wait. Jake would have this forty cleared before the end of the year. She was hoping she would be expecting again soon.

The thought of growing their family made Marina think about space. With a guilty glance over at Jake, who had laid the paper aside and was half asleep, she slipped her finger in beside the strand of thread she used for a bookmark and turned to the section labeled, *Sears Modern Homes*.

Sears could ship an entire house to you by boxcar. All you had to do was put it together when it arrived. How simple! Longingly, Marina poured over the house plans. The Hillrose was two stories high with five bedrooms, a dining room, living room, AND a parlor! What would you do with a house that big?

Conscience-stricken, Marina snapped the catalogue shut. Nothing from Sears would be as nice as what Jake would build for their family. Perhaps they could get a place of their own in a couple of years.

She stood up. "Let's go to bed," she invited her husband.

September 6, 1915

"It's a girl!" Dr. Franklin announced. "Mother and child are doing fine."

Jake heaved a sigh of relief. He had thought it would get easier the second time around, but several more babies would arrive before he finally accepted the fact that Marina giving birth would never be a comfortable experience—for either of them.

April 6, 1917

"America is officially at war," Jake announced, sitting down at the kitchen table.

Marina sat across from him, instinctively hugging two-year-old Flora and reaching out to touch three-year-old Rosa Lee's head. For a moment she wondered if it might not be best to have all girls so they would never have to worry about one of their children going to war. Reassured by the physical touch, she found her voice. "Does this really have to involve us? Germany, England, Japan. . ., they're all so far away from here."

"According to the papers, Germany's still bombing our passenger ships."

Marina smoothed Rosa Lee's hair back from her eyes. "Well, can't we just keep our boats out of those waters until Europeans have settled their differences? We have everything we need right here in the United States."

"According to Clifton Sawyer over at the feed store, we're already involved. He says he knows for a fact German spies have infiltrated U.S. labor unions, stealing secrets from our factories and setting fire to warehouses in New York City."

"How does he know that for a fact?" Marina questioned.

"He got a letter from his cousin Finis Sawyer, who lives right across the river in New Jersey. Finis sent Clifton copies of the New York papers that say the Germans have sabotaged dozens of factories just in their city. There's talk a network of secret German agents are poisonin' water supplies and kidnappin' U.S. citizens. I'm not quite sure I believe that one. What would the German government want with a bunch of ordinary citizens?"

Marina shook her head and patted Flora on the back. "I'm glad we live in Arkansas where that ugliness can't touch us or harm the girls. New York's got a lot of people livin' up there. They should be able to manage a handful of Germans."

Jake nodded, not completely convinced Arkansas was isolated from the effects of a world war. "Some of the young men around Manila have already joined up. Jess Pierce did. So did Clifton Sawyer's boy. Both of the Eckridge sons enlisted."

Tired of the talk about German spies and Manila boys going overseas, Marina began clearing the table. "Did you notice how well my garden's doin'?"

"Yes, ma'am. I'm lookin' forward to all those fresh vegetables." He stood up and kissed his wife before heading out to the fields. He knew a hint when he heard one.

Chapter Eight

August 1918

Guiding Rosa Lee by the hand, Marina maneuvered her way through the cramped aisles of Fendler's Grocery. The store was a maze of loaded shelves, stacked boxes, and glass-topped display cases. She held hands with Flora while keeping her free hand on top of Rosa Lee's head so she could turn the little girl's face whichever direction she wanted her to go. Marina turned first to the left so as not to bump into Mrs. Pendergrass, who was shopping for knitting needles, and then pulled Rosa Lee to the right so the little girl wouldn't be stepped on by Rufus Tillman.

Everybody within ten miles of Manila must be in town tonight, she thought. The war had everybody keyed up. Even the mood of shoppers seemed different. People were restless instead of bustling. Out in the streets angry voices rose, slurred with liquid confidence and stirred by personal grudges. The sun may have gone down, but it sure felt as if the heat was scorching the cotton, the vegetables, and people's attitudes too.

A spirited boy popped his head around the aisle and grinned at her, "Miz Hartmann," he greeted her.

"Well, Oscar Fendler, how are you? I can't believe how big you've grown! I sure wouldn't be able to catch you runnin' down the street now. You must be such a help to your mother."

"Yes, ma'am." Oscar ducked his head and grinned.

"How are you doin' in school?"

"Not more'n one fight a day," he bragged. "Used to be two, but I cut back on account of the whuppin's."

Marina nodded gravely, careful not to offend his sense of accomplishment. "Do you think you could cut it down to one every other day?"

"I don't know how's that would be possible," he admitted frankly. "You see, we're fightin' a war at school, and they need me. Used to be Cowboys and Indians, but now it's the Allies and the Germans. I'm the general of the German army on account of my family's real German Jews." His pride in his family's status as immigrants was obvious. "We Germans win most of the time." He lowered his voice and confided. "That's 'cuz I always pick the biggest boys."

"Good plan."

"Look over there," he jerked his head toward the next aisle. Marina cut her eyes to the right. "That's the Allies' general."

"I see."

The leader of the recess playground Allies worked his way over to them. "You Germans are goin' down on Monday," he announced.

"Yeah?" Oscar's voice rose in excitement. "We Germans won't rest until every last one of you Allies is dead." Seven-year-old Oscar cheerfully delivered his threat.

The reaction from adults across the store was immediate. Stunned silence turned ominous and then exploded with emotion.

"We'll see about that!" an angry man with a red, pinched-looking face retorted. Before the man was out the door, they could hear him bellow to his friends, "Hey, Brimer! Did you hear what that Hun in there is sayin'? He says they won't rest until every Ally is dead."

Confused, Oscar turned to his playmate. "Has he got a boy on your side?"

"Oscar, hush!" his mother commanded from behind the counter.

Customers hurried out of the store. Some people simply didn't want to be part of such an uncomfortable moment; others went in search of a buddy to whom they could repeat the story and perhaps add a little salt and pepper. A few left visibly shaken by the feel of violence in the air.

Marina shivered though the air was humid. She quietly finished gathering her groceries and proceeded to the counter. The night had turned ugly, and she wanted to be home.

Sounds of the crowd milling around the street bubbled like a hot pot on the verge of scorching. Shoppers shuffled from store to store at a faster pace. Curiously, no one new entered Fendler's Grocery. Marina could hear her own voice struggling to lighten the atmosphere. Mrs. Fendler responded to customers' questions, grateful for polite conversations, but too distracted to participate in them. Young Oscar resumed stocking the shelves, aware he had stirred up something but too unseasoned to understand what.

The rhythm of the town had skidded offbeat. Disquietude over the Great War agitated the air people breathed. Most families had come to town to get away from reality, to escape the repetitive farm tasks that left too much time for thinking. They came craving the voices of other parents who would reassure them that the boys were taking care of business and would all be home safely within a couple of months. Now, they were caught up in a swirl of parental protectiveness tainted by prejudice. Fear had stiffened opinions into hardness of heart.

Outside, men were spouting bigotry disguised as patriotism. The shop door, propped open earlier in the day to encourage patronage, now seemed to almost invite hostility as if flaunting their supposedly evil intentions in downtown Manila.

Marina felt torn between a desire to flee with her little girls and a responsibility to stay and provide Mrs. Fendler some measure of comfort. All the other shoppers had disappeared.

86

Both women turned to look when a shadow slipped up the steps leading to the store. Marina was relieved to see Jake appear in the doorway. He scanned the store to verify the safety of his family before focusing in on Mrs. Fendler.

"They say Oscar's talkin' 'bout defeatin' the Allies."

"He's talkin' 'bout school yard fights, not the war," the boy's mother protested.

"That may be, but people with sons in the war are hearin' German sympathy. They think he's spoutin' anti-American talk he's learned at home."

"That's silly," Marina dismissed it.

"That's dangerous," Jake corrected.

Marina drew her children closer as Jake continued. "Miz Fendler, I think you and Oscar best call it an evenin'. I'll close up the store for you."

Rebecca Fendler nodded. "We'll go on home, then."

Jake hesitated. Mrs. Fendler looked so thin and defenseless. She had never completely recovered from that bout with Malaria. "I'm not sure it would be a good idea for you to go to your home, ma'am."

"No, it wouldn't," a voice concurred. Gabriel Mikes, Lebanese owner of a competing store down the street, entered from the back of the building. His curly black hair was cropped close to his head. He had thick eyebrows above a kind but tired face. "It's gettin' ugly out there. My house is only about a hundred yards from here. I don't think we can risk taking them any farther, but we've got to get them out of here. Come on, Rebecca."

Rebecca Fendler hesitated, glancing around at the stacks of merchandise still needing to be shelved. She always straightened the store before leaving. "Come on, Rebecca," Garbriel encouraged. "We need to go now. There's not much time."

"Not much time before what?" Distress clouded the woman's thin face.

Worried, Gabriel spoke faster. "Not much time before a mob forms. Can't you hear them talkin' in the streets? Mickey Jarvis and Ervin Eskridge are roundin' up a bunch of their drinkin' buddies. They're spoutin' some nonsense about defendin' their town. It's a good thing your husband is away pickin' up merchandise in Memphis. Seeing a male German Jew might really incite them. This way, Rebecca. We'll go out the back."

Miz Fendler's hand shook visibly as she laid it on Oscar's shoulder. She nodded her thanks at Jake and followed Mr. Mikes out the back door.

Jake reached behind the counter. He had the heavy key in hand when a stampede of heavy boots and loud voices erupted into the room. "Where are they?" angry voices shouted.

"Where are who?" Jake asked, his calm voice hiding the fact he was desperately stalling for time.

"You know who I'm talkin' 'bout," a three-hundred-pound man with a thick beard roared. "Those Kaiser-lovin' Jews. Bring 'em out here. We're gonna string 'em up. We'll teach 'em to breed Krauts right here in the middle of the U.S.A."

Marina stood stock still. She recognized three of the six men: Noland Richards, Floyd Lasiter, and Mickey Jarvis. Any other day she wouldn't have worried about a one of them: a business owner and a couple of farmers, all family men. Tonight, bound together by drink, suspicion, and a frustrating knowledge they were helpless to do anything about the war, they fed off each other's agitation.

Jake spread his hands in a gesture of openness. "As you can see, they're not here."

"They were here twenty minutes ago," the man with the pinched face insisted. "You must be hidin' 'em."

"You're welcome to search," Jake invited.

The men spread out. One man charged behind the curtain to the back room. Another scrutinized the space behind the counter, opening cabinets too small to hide a dog. A third stomped through each aisle, kicking at boxes, intentionally knocking produce off the shelves.

"Where are they?" the big man blustered, inflamed by Jake's calmness.

"Maybe he doesn't want to tell us," Noland Richards sneered. "Maybe he wants 'em to get away, eh, Hartmann? Come to think of it, we don't know much about you. Your family got any German blood?"

Jake took his time as if considering the question carefully. "Don't rightly know," he finally concluded. "Should we assume I do?"

"Aww, Jake ain't no Kaiser-lover," Mickey interrupted. "I bet those Germans are already slidin' out a town. Let's go block off the ends of Baltimore Street. We can check every wagon that passes."

"Yeah!" The men were more zealous about the fact that they had a new plan than they were concerned whether or not it was a good one. They left as fast as they had entered.

Jake waited until he heard their horses trotting away. "You alright?" he asked Marina.

"Yes, we're fine. Let's just get home."

Jake shook his head. "We can't get home tonight. There's no tellin' what those boys'll do when they start checkin' wagons. I'll take you to your mother's on the edge of town and then come back up here in case I'm needed. Tomorrow they'll be sleepin' it off. They won't be such fools in broad daylight."

Marina nodded. She was tired beyond the physical and at this moment there was no one she wanted to see as much as her mother.

Jake locked up the store, commenting that doing so felt pretty worthless because if those troublemakers wanted to come back, a locked door would only feed their desire to get in. Marina held Flora tight and climbed onto the spring seat of the wagon. Jake lifted Rosa Lee onto the seat beside her. Marina cuddled her girls, praying for safety and wishing there was a way to protect them from life's ugliness.

The next morning Marina and Hattie were sitting at the kitchen table when Jake opened the screen door. Without a word, Hattie poured another cup of black coffee and set it down in front of him.

"What's the news in town?" Marina prompted. "Are the Fendlers alright?'

"The Fendlers are fine. The Dodds, who own the mercantile across the street from them, didn't fair so well."

"The Dodds?" Marina repeated. "Why? What do they have to do with it? Both sets of their grandparents were born right here in Mississippi County."

"Yes, but they've been accused of having German sympathies."

"Those men didn't hurt them, did they?"

"Somebody painted their entire storefront yellow." Jake shook his head. "It's a mess."

"That's awful! Is the sheriff going to arrest them?"

"Arrest who?" Jake asked. "Nobody saw anybody do anything."

"Why, arrest those men who came to the store last night!" Marina's voice was indignant. "Didn't you tell the sheriff?"

"Sure. But the sheriff doesn't know if it's the same people. Besides, Marina, we didn't see them do anything illegal. They showed up at the store during business hours, asked for the owners, and left when they didn't find them. Not a thing you can put a man in jail for."

"They were drunk!"

"So was a quarter of the town. The sheriff never would get his work done if he locked up every man in town who had too much to drink on Saturday night."

"He wouldn't get re-elected neither," Hattie commented.

Jake grinned. "No, ma'am, I don't guess he would."

Chapter Nine

September, 1918

T he bedroom door opened and Hattie popped her head out to give the news. "It's a boy, Jake." Hattie cradled her first grandson in her arms. "He looks like you. Are you going to call him 'Jacob'?"

"Nah! He needs his own name. I like the name 'Walter.' That sounds like a strong man who'll accomplish things. Let's call him that."

"He may be his own man, but he'll have the character of his pappy," Marina predicted proudly from the other side of the wall. "Girls," she called to Rosa Lee and Flora who were peeking around the corner, "Come meet your brother."

November 11, 1918

Jake exited the barn and spotted Marina digging up plants for the third move. Discouraged, he walked toward her. "Marina," he began awkwardly. "I'm sorry you have to keep diggin' up your plants every time I start clearin' a new forty. I didn't think it would take me this long to buy some land."

"That's okay, Jake," Marina gave him a cheerful smile. "This is only temporary. One day, we'll have a home of our own. And then," Marina paused for emphasis, "I won't *ever* dig these plants up again. Unless it's to divide them for transplanting," she added realistically.

He stared at the plants. "Where's baby Walter?"

"Inside with Rosa Lee. It's a little too chilly out here for him." Marina smiled. "That girl is a natural-born mother. I'm beginning to think she knows when he's hungry or wet before he does."

Jake smiled and started to reply, but was interrupted by the sound of feet running towards them.

"Jake, Marina!" a young man's voice yelled.

Marina looked up to see her youngest brother, Noel, running full steam towards them. His face was puffed red. "Jake, Marina!" he called again, softly this time now that he could see them.

She stood up, fear gripping her heart as she moved toward him. Something must have happened to one of the boys or to

Mama. "What is it, Noel? What's happened?" He was so out of breath he couldn't respond. She put her hand on his arm, resisting the urge to shake the news out of him.

"It's all right, Noel. Catch your breath," Jake instructed.

The boy let out big breaths, each one successively less, and then nodded. "It's. . .over," he panted. "The Great War. . .is. . .over."

Jake let out a yell. He picked up his wife, swinging her around.

It took a moment for Marina's mind to register what Noel was saying. "The war?" she repeated. "Then Mama and the boys are alright?" she asked, still focused on her family.

"They're better'n alright. They're celebratin'. The county's celebratin'. Hang it all, Marina, the whole world's celebratin'!"

Immense relief flooded her. Her own world was still secure. "It's over," she repeated softly. "The Great War is over! We've finished the war to end all wars. Our son and my brothers will never have to fight a war. It's over."

"Well, if the whole world is celebratin', we'd better join 'em," Jake suggested.

December 25, 1918

Marina stood at the kitchen, counter spreading the final swirls on a chocolate cake. Out the window she could see five-year-old Rosa Lee and three-year-old Flora traipsing out to the barn after Jake. Automatically, her eyes went to the tiny cradle to check on Walter—a mother hen always counting her chicks. The girls kept looking back to the house and dissolving into giggles. They followed Jake inside the barn.

A few minutes later the trio emerged again. The girls were laughing out loud. Not even Jake could keep the wide smile off his face. Had it been any other day but Christmas, Marina would have gone to investigate.

Finally, the three huddled in a circle, a team forming a plan. Jake pointed them towards the house, then wheeled around to head back into the barn. Flora sprinted towards her mother, a clear attempt to be the first to share good news. Rosa Lee raced behind her pleading, "Not yet, Flora, not yet! Pappy's not ready." Stifling her smile, Marina turned to the sink and was nonchalantly washing dishes when they burst through the door.

"Mommy!" Flora exclaimed.

"Yes, Flora?"

"Nothing, nothing," Rosa Lee did her best to intervene, but Flora continued.

"We got a present for you! It's big!"

Desperate to stop her little sister, Rosa Lee tugged her by the arm. "Let's go back and help Pappy." She pulled Flora from the room while instructing her mother. "Mommy, you take Walter in the bedroom because. . .because he needs you. We'll call you when. . .when we need you. Stay in there, Mommy. Don't look out the window. Promise?"

"I promise," Marina laughed. She scooped up Walter and walked back to the bedroom. "What on earth are they up to?" she asked him. She hoped they'd hurry. She had a lot more to do if she was going to get dinner on the table by noon.

Moments later, she heard the door slam. She could hear shuffling and something heavy being scooted into place across the floor. Then, Flora's voice rang out, "Ready! Close your eyes. Your present is ready for you."

"Let's go, Walter." Marina told her son. "You don't want to miss the surprise either, do you?"

"Look, Mommy!" her girls shouted, standing in front of a big cabinet. "We bought you a sewing machine!"

"A sewing machine?" Marina glanced at Jake for confirmation.

He wore the biggest smile she had ever seen. "I ordered it from Sears and had it sent to your mother's house. Your brothers brought it over today. We hid it in the barn."

Marina knelt down beside the machine, gently running her hand over the top. Her gift was shiny black with gleaming metal. Lotus decals gave it an almost exotic look.

When she didn't say anything, Jake began to get nervous. "We can't afford the house yet, but I've been saving to get this Singer for you."

Still no response as she scrutinized every inch of the black machine. A side compartment contained the manual and spare spools. One by one she took out the attachments, noting their size and shape, trying to imagine what each one was capable of doing.

"I wanted you to be surprised. Do you like it?" Marina pushed the treadle with her foot, so deep in her thoughts that his voice sounded as if it came to her from far off.

She tore herself away from the machine to hug the girls. Then she threw her arms around Jake. Oh, yes, yes! I love it!"

"Mommy, thank Walter too. It's from all of us," Rosa Lee explained.

Marina dropped a kiss on the baby's forehead, then turned back to Jake. "I've never had anything like it before. I can't wait to sew dresses for the girls and shirts and pants for you and Walter as soon as he's big enough to wear them."

"No more sewin' clothes by hand!" Jake declared.

"Do you think I can learn how to use it?"

"Of course you can. The catalogue says it practically sews clothes by itself."

Manual in hand, she looked at the diagram and then back at her machine to identify each part. "That's the presser foot and the presser bar lift. Oh, the bobbin goes down in there out of sight. The balance wheel always has to turn toward me. That makes sense. I see how to thread it. Look at that! I can change the size of the stitch by turnin' the thumb screw — to the right to lengthen — to the left to shorten. It even hems! And you can use it to stitch on lace. Oh, Jake, the girls have to have a dress with lace on it! And ruffles! Rosa Lee! Flora! See this? I can use it to sew ruffles on your dress. Do you girls know what ruffles are? You've never had them. Jake, it guides the needle so the stitchin' line stays straight! Did you ever see anythin' like it?" Marina stood up. "I'll get started on the girls' dresses right away."

"Mommy, I hungry," Flora protested.

"I forgot all about dinner," Marina confessed.

Chapter Ten

September 1920

"Anybody home?" Cousin Eddie's voice called from the screen door.

Marina didn't answer and made a face at Jake when he yelled, "Come on in, Eddie."

The door squeaked and Eddie strode into the house. "For a moment there, I thought you might be out in the field. Oh, good, I'm just in time for coffee. That is one thing you do right, Marina. You boil a good cup of coffee. Don't mind if I do have one."

Jake noticed coffee wasn't the only thing boiling in the kitchen and guided the conversation in a new direction. "What are you doing out this way, Eddie?"

"Just dropped in on Aunt Hattie. It's good she and the boys moved out here closer to you'uns since Doc died. Now *there*," Eddie jabbed his finger in the air, "was a great man. Yes, sir,

Doc was one of a kind. A great one!" Eddie glanced around the kitchen. "That sausage looks mighty good."

Marina took two sausage patties off the serving plate sitting on the stove and set them down in front of Eddie with a cup of coffee.

Jake drank the last sip of his coffee. He was anxious to get logging but didn't want to leave his wife at the mercy of her cousin's pushiness. "What kind of work are you doin' these days, Ed?"

"Oh, little of this, little of that," he avoided the question. "I've got several possibilities I'm considerin'." Eddie switched the subject. "Herman Davis got home from the war last week. They say he's a war hero—one of the top five in the entire country. There's rumors he keeps a bunch of medals in his fishin' tackle box, even one from the French. I don't much believe it. Herman was always too quiet, hardly ever said a word in school."

"Bein' quiet could be a good thing if you was sneakin' up on the enemy," Jake observed. "Herman's a good hunter. Those men from up in Chicago pay him a lot of money to guide them around Big Lake."

"Yeah, but that's different. That's duck huntin'. We're talkin' 'bout fightin' the Germans."

"Bigger target," Marina muttered just loud enough to be heard. Jake looked down at his empty mug so no one could see him chuckle. Marina never had forgiven Eddie for tricking her into trying to vote.

"Could I have another cup of coffee, Marina?" Eddie sighed as if weary of having to ask for it. "Did you hear the news? Women have got the vote now. Don't that just beat all? What are they goin' to do 'cept vote whichever way their husband tells them to vote." Eddie's opinion was met with silence which he interpreted as an invitation to continue in a louder voice. "That means ever' married man's goin' to get two votes while the vote of a single man like myself will count only once. Nothin' fair about it, simple math, but I guess those hand pressers in Washington can't count that high." He drummed his fingers on the table, seemingly bored with his own conversation. "Marina, you goin' to vote?"

Suddenly absorbed in stripping chicken off the bones of Sunday's leftovers, Marina turned her face toward the counter. That old shame and humiliation flooded over her. "No, I don't believe I will," she answered in a small voice.

Eddie nodded his approval, "That's as it should be. You women best leave the decision-making to us men folks." He grinned. "You learned that a long time ago, didn't you, Marina?"

Jake stood, "Ed, why don't you come on out and see how much progress we've made clearin' land. I'll even let you swing the axe a couple of times."

At the mention of hard labor, Eddie jumped up, shaking the table and spilling his still-full coffee into the saucer. "I'd like to, but I'd better get on home. Momma'll be needin' me to. . . .She'll be wantin' me to. . .do somethin'."

That's a truer statement than he intended, Marina thought to herself.

"You sure?" Jake baited him. "Fellin' trees is a great way to build up an appetite."

"Nope, nope," Eddie couldn't reach the door fast enough. "Can't keep Momma waitin'. Wouldn't be fair."

"In that case," Jake smiled, "I'll walk you out."

Marina put a pot of broth on the stove, mixed up some dough for dumplin's, and then spent the morning scooping out pumpkin, cutting it into chunks, and canning it. Jake came in for the noon meal. As soon as he returned to logging, she readied the children and they set out on the walk to her mother's cabin. By cutting across fallow fields they shortened the walk to one mile.

The farm near town where her Mama had lived since her husband had died was owned jointly by Doc and his brothers. It had been part of the men's inheritance from old Moses Bauer. As long as her father was alive, Hattie and her sons could live there without rent and without paying the landowner fifty percent of the harvest.

Now that Doc was gone, the remaining brothers wanted to rent the property to a paying tenant. Once again, the death of the male closest to her had caused Hattie to lose her home. Marina hated that her mother had always had to work like a man.

She also felt sorry about the loss of the farm. That was where she and Jake had courted. On the other hand, she loved having her mother sharecrop close by. On easy days like this she could get her own work done in the morning, spend the afternoon with Hattie, and still be home in time to have supper ready for Jake. Her mother had sent Noel over to say they had harvested corn yesterday. She wanted to help her mother can.

The children played outside while Hattie and Marina worked. Side by side, sometimes silent, sometimes chatting, the two women enjoyed the leisure of not having to rush a conversation. They shucked the cobs, blanched the ears, and then sliced off the kernels. They had just begun the process of filling the quart jars when they were interrupted.

Marina and Hattie heard the scuffle before they saw it. The screen door shot open slamming the wooden frame against the wall. Both women turned to see what the commotion was about. Walter stood there, chubby little legs planted shoulder width apart. Tall for his age, he presented a forceful little representation of manliness. Flora stood behind him, hair disarrayed, brown eyes blazing with fury, and feet itching to stomp a storm. Rosa Lee, always the peacemaker, entered last, anxious and clearly distressed that she could not placate her siblings.

"Mommy," Walter demanded, "tell Flora she's got to do what I say 'cause I'm the man."

Marina looked her precious son in the eye and for the briefest second saw the tiny bit of Eddie that exists in every man. "You're the man, alright," Marina confirmed with a light

104

swat on his rear. "Now go bring in some wood for Grandma's stove. Her stack is gettin' low."

Walt obeyed, with Rosa Lee following to make sure he didn't get hurt. Flora continued to stand there. "He's just a boy anyway," the girl fussed.

Marina bit her lip to keep from smiling. "Flora, take the crock and pump Grandma some fresh water." Reluctantly, Flora collected the pitcher. Mother and Grandmother watched the next generation carry out her chore, waiting until she was out of earshot before they looked at each other and began to laugh.

The last hours of their visit passed without further calamity. "Well, Mama, I've enjoyed the visit. Rosa Lee, Flora, Walter, let's go," Marina called. "I need to fix supper before your pappy comes in." She kissed her mother goodbye and they trudged off down the road.

When they finally arrived home, Marina started pulling the meal together. She opened a quart of vegetable soup. That just needed warming up. She lit the stove and then dumped a couple cups of flour into a bowl. Before long she was pressing a jar lid into the dough to cut out biscuits. Rosa Lee busied herself opening a pint of homemade applesauce and heating up a quart of corn.

"Flora, set the table for supper, please."

The screen door slammed. "That sure smells good," Jake announced, walking in.

"It'll be ready in five minutes," Marina promised.

"It'll take me just about that long to clean up."

"Mommy," Flora tugged on her mother's apron. "Will you fix sweet potatoes for supper?"

"I don't have any sweet potatoes, honey."

"I do." Flora held up a large, dirty sweet potato.

Marina took the orange root from her. "Where did you get a sweet potato?"

"From Grandma's house."

"I didn't see Grandma give you a sweet potato."

"I took it—from her garden."

"Without permission?" Marina was aghast.

Flora stared at her. Finally, she nodded very slowly.

"Flora, that's stealin'! You can't take somethin' that doesn't belong to you."

"I like sweet potatoes," Flora explained.

"It doesn't matter. You still can't take things that don't belong to you. We're goin' to take it back, and you're goin' to tell Grandma that you are very, very sorry. Then you are never goin' to steal anything again. Is that clear, young lady?"

"Yes, ma'am." Flora's lip trembled and her eyes filled with tears.

Jake walked back into the kitchen in time to hear the gist of what had happened. "You go on back to your Mama's before it starts getting dark. I'll take care of these two." He kissed Marina and patted Flora's shoulder in encouragement.

It was a long trip back to Hattie's. Flora did her best to lag behind until Marina finally took her by the hand. "Flora, there is no point in draggin' it out. Let's hurry. You'll feel better once you have made everything right with Grandma."

Flora still dawdled. "I didn't mean to steal," she protested, tears coming once more.

Marina turned to face her daughter. She felt as miserable as the little girl did. "I know you didn't mean to, but the point is you did. It doesn't matter if you're in a store or in somebody's house. If you take somethin' that doesn't belong to you, it's stealin'."

"But she had so many."

"Yes, and they were hers, not yours."

Distressed, Flora nodded, and the two continued their journey.

When they finally arrived, Hattie was coming up the path from the barn where she had been milking the cow. "Is everything all right?" she called.

"No, Mama, everything is not all right. Flora has something to say to you." She nudged the little girl forward.

Hattie came closer, kneeling down beside her granddaughter. She put one arm around her, concern evident in her voice. "What's the matter, honey?"

Flora held up the sweet potato. "I took it from your garden without askin'."

Hattie understood this was a character-forming moment and accepted the sweet potato with a grave face. "Thank you for bringin' it back. Would you tell me why you took it?"

"Because I *really* like sweet potatoes, and we didn't have any at home."

"I would have given you all the sweet potatoes you wanted if you had asked me. Well, you did the right thing in bringin' it back. Next time you want a sweet potato, you ask Grandma. Alright, Flora?"

"Yes, ma'am."

Hattie reached out, pulling Flora into a loving embrace. Then standing up, she addressed her daughter. "Do you want to come in for a cup of coffee, Marina?"

"We'd better get on home. It's been a long day. Jake and the other children will be waitin' for their supper."

Hattie nodded. As Marina and Flora started down the road, she called out, "You're a good mother, Marina."

Chapter Eleven

October 1920

Twilight was Marina's favorite time of day. She loved the hour when the last dish had been dried and put away, the children were scrubbed, clothes prepared for the next day, and life was in order.

She and Jake often sat on the front porch talking, their hands busy cracking nuts, shelling a pan of beans, or some other task. They shared whatever news from town they chanced to hear, repeated anything funny the children had said, and estimated the price of cotton. And always, always, they dreamed about a house of their own: how big the rooms would be, how close the water pump, and how convenient a two-seater out-house would be. Their childhoods had been rocky and they both had a desire for permanency, a need to feel secure, and immovably home.

Even after the last rays of sun had soaked into the Arkansas soil, the family would sit on the porch a few minutes longer, cocooned in the darkness, children occasionally popping down the steps to chase frogs. Then, reluctantly, understanding he was breaking a magic spell, Jake would say, "Time to go to bed. Tomorrow's goin' to be a long day."

Rosa Lee continued to be a great help to her mother. She loved to cook and take care of her brother and sister. Marina could picture her grown with a great gaggle of her own babies. Flora was confident and smart as a whip, eagerly trooping off to school every morning, pouring over her books at night, and soaking up everything anyone said. Walter, the little man, worked the pump like a logger. He trotted in with stove kindling piled higher than his head. He idolized his father, constantly looking for new ways to imitate his hero's mannerisms and walk.

"You 'bout done with that dress, Marina?"

Surprised, Marina looked up from the sewing machine. "I'm workin' on the sleeves." Whatever Jake had to tell, it was good news. As nonchalant as he was trying to be, he could not hide that smile. She sat back in her chair and waited for him to continue.

That was all the encouragement he needed. "I found it," he announced.

"What did you find?" she asked, trying to remember what had been lost.

"The land where we're goin' to build a house of our own."

"Our land? A home for our family? Where?"

"Two miles south of here."

"How can we afford it?"

"I've got that all worked out. We'll buy it on time. The whole forty acres is virgin timber. Money from the lumber will cover payments until the cotton comes in. We'll plant corn to feed the animals. We need a cash crop, so I'll clear ten acres for cotton. We can use enough wood to build our house and a barn. The limbs from the trees will provide enough fuel for two years. That should give us a good start. Each year I'll clear more land until we're farmin' the whole forty acres. It's flatland. We won't lose an inch of plantin' space to hills. This is good land, Marina, good farm soil that goes down as far as I can dig."

Jake leaned forward. "I'll build you a big four-room house, Marina. Kitchen, living room, two bedrooms. Plenty of room for a family of five."

"Make that a family of six," Marina corrected.

"Six?" Jake's eyebrows shot up and then he laughed. "I hope it's a boy. We could use another man on the Hartmann Farm."

. . .

Marina relished every moment of her first trip to their land. She loved going farther south into the forest. Mississippi County was being cleared so fast that the beautiful woods of her childhood were disappearing.

111

Jake gave his family the grand tour as if he already knew every foot of their acreage. "I was thinkin' the house could face west so's we can watch the sun set of an evenin'."

Marina took a deep breath and dreamed. "Imagine shellin' peas on our own front porch." The sound of gleeful shrieking brought her back to reality. She glanced over at the children scattering through the trees and instructed, "Don't go far! Stay within the sound of your pappy's whistle."

Seeing that they were minding, Jake continued. "The house can sit right here behind that old oak. I can cut the tree down to make more space."

"Oh, no, Jake," Marina protested. "That's a fine oak. Promise me you'll leave it. Since the land is ours, we don't have to cut down every tree as sharecroppers do."

Jake shrugged. "We can leave it. You'll still have plenty of room for a large garden on the south side of the house. Your tomatoes will soak up the hot afternoon sun."

Marina nodded, mentally planting her vegetables. "I can garden a bigger plot this year. That'll also leave plenty of room for my flowers. I want a mess of flowers leadin' up the path and runnin' 'round the foundation of our house."

Jake laughed. "You are going to leave me a little room to plant some cotton, aren't you?"

"Maybe a little," she conceded. "I'd like a good-sized front porch."

"You'll have it," he promised. With long strides Jake walked off the blueprint in his head. Marina smiled approvingly and he continued. "Behind that clump of buttonbush is a good spot for the chicken house."

"I can tie my clothesline up on those two maples," she pointed, "and run it even with the garden."

"We can put a wash house out just behind it. I'll build in plenty of shelves for your cannin' jars. Next summer, Walt and I will start on a barn."

A string of ducks flew across the sky. Marina watched them circle for a moment, then with a resilience reminiscent of her mother's Cherokee ancestors, she announced, "I don't care what the government or those sports up at the clubhouse say. When they fly over our land, those are our ducks!"

Jake grinned.

"Where are you goin' to put the pump?" she asked.

"Good question." He strode over to Marina's oak, as he now thought of the tree. Whipping out his pocket knife, he cut off a Y-shaped fork. Elbows tight against his abdomen, Jake held the two ends loosely in his hands with the third end pointing straight out and began to walk. The children stopped playing to watch. Methodically, Jake rounded what would be the footprint of their house. He went around three or four times, each rectangle clearing a little wider path. When he was about fifteen feet out from where they planned the south wall, the end of the stick began to dip. He continued letting the divining rod guide him as the end dipped lower and lower. When the stick pointed straight down he stopped. "Right here," he announced. "Flora, run get me that wellpoint from the back of the wagon."

Flora ran to obey and returned with a pipe two inches in diameter and sixty inches long. The family continued watching as Jake's strong muscles drove the point into the ground. He pulled a screw and some string out of his pocket, which he tied together. Then he lowered the weighted string down the center of the pipe. When he brought the string back up, it was wet. "There's your water." He put a cap over the top. "Next time I'm out here, I'll put the pump on."

Jake dusted the dirt off his hands. "Let's walk across our land," he invited. The children weaved around them while they walked. Marina kept getting distracted with the plants she identified. Wild mushrooms climbed old stumps and growing trees. Small, mitten-shaped leaves promised enough sassafras for whatever ails you. "Juniper berries! We always need those when Rosa Lee gets an upset stomach or Walt gets covered in bug bites. Girls, look at this. See these shiny leaves? We'll be pickin' elderberries in September. Look at all this! We're going to have chokeberries, huckleberries, blackberries, and even your favorite, Walt,—blueberries. See those triangle-shaped leaves? It's a greenbrier shrub. You have to watch out for large thorns on that one."

"Mommy, look over there!" Rosa Lee pointed to a miniature meadow located on a slight rise of the land. There in the middle

114

of the clearing, giant wild sunflowers strained their faces to the sun and swayed in the breeze. They looked like dancers listening to the forest's song. Secluded, in the center of a virgin wood, it appeared God had planted them for His Own delight.

"It's beautiful, Rosa Lee." Amazed, they stood there for a moment. "It really doesn't look as if they'd have enough sun to grow in that patch of grass. How strange! Well, sometimes things just bloom where they're not supposed to."

"Mommy," Walt called for her attention. "I hear water. Is that from Pappy's pump?"

Marina smiled, thinking it was his imagination and then realized she too could hear water flowing. She looked over at Jake, who was grinning broadly.

"I have a surprise for you," he announced. "Come this way."

The family followed him as he beat a path through their personal forest, around bushes, over fallen logs, and up a slight ridge, all the while drawing nearer to the sound of moving water. At the top of the ridge, they looked down. Not more than ten feet below them, Little River ran along the east side of their land.

"Little River flows out of Big Lake. That's kind of like givin' you back your childhood home, isn't it?" Jake asked.

Marina squeezed his arm. "Buildin' my life here with you is much better."

"Look at all the fish!" Walt yelled.

Black bass could be seen gliding through the water. "Pappy, I see a turtle," Flora called. Sure enough, a red-ear slider turtle was creeping its way along the bank.

"Pappy and I can fish every night. Mommy, you don't ever have to plant a garden again."

Marina smiled. "Maybe we should still plant a few things like corn and watermelon."

"Okay," Walt agreed, "but no broccoli. There's no need for broccoli."

Chapter Twelve

Autumn 1920

C learing his own land was pure joy. Jake had always been an early riser, but now he was up before the sun even considered rising. A quick breakfast and he was out the door. At noon time, he came in for a shortened dinner break, then back outside, where he worked until it was too dark to continue. He still put in a full week's worth of sharecropping, but every moment that could be spared was dedicated to their future home.

Marina's delight matched his. She sent Rosa Lee and Flora out to him with jugs of coffee to keep his energy flowing. She pulled out cotton sacks she'd been saving and made curtains for the new windows. Rosa Lee, Flora, and Walter went with her to the cotton fields, where she spent more time than ever providing Jake with additional hours for sawing lumber.

Her mind was always on the new house even as she buzzed about her regular chores. While she hung up laundry outside the sharecropping bungalow, she pictured her future garden, analyzing the best location for each vegetable. When feeding the chickens, she determined who would sleep where in the new house. She realized they needed new mattresses. She had the ticking, but not enough stuffing. Her eyes lit on a flock of geese flying overhead, and the family had roasted goose for Thanksgiving instead of turkey.

In the evening, the family sat out on the porch, she and Jake in rockers pulled out from the living room, their children perched nearby. Conversation had changed. Instead of the future, they talked about the present — what had been accomplished on the land, their land, that day.

. . .

By March, he had cleared four acres. From the river running along the east side of their property, Jake selected nine boulders. With the use of old scrap wood, he rolled the boulders into the wheelbarrow for transport home. Using a chisel, he flattened opposite sides to fashion three support stones down each side and three across the middle.

Marina and the children were planting squash in the new garden when the first beam went up. A red-tailed hawk screamed overhead. Marina stood there with a catch in her throat, watching the wood and her dream rise to the sky. "Look, Rosa Lee, Flora, Walt!" The children cheered and she laughed. "Let's get back to the garden. We need to work as hard as your pappy does."

Jake timed their move with the completion of the sharecropping season in late October. When he started a job, he finished it and never considered leaving Clay with crops in the field.

Marina transplanted her flowers and bushes two days before they moved in. "There ought to be a drum roll," she called to Jake as she and the children paraded greenery from the wagon to their new home. He obliged by beating on a two-by-four.

Moving day arrived. By dawn they were loading the wagon with everything Marina and Rosa Lee had packed the night before. Only her black iron skillet still sat on the stove. For breakfast she fried eggs "with the bubble in the middle" as her children called them. She added thick slices of home-cured bacon, wrapped them in buttermilk biscuits, and served oozy sandwiches. They were so good even delicate Rosa Lee licked her fingers before washing at the pump.

The joy of owning their land held fast. Weeding, or choppin' cotton, as they called it, felt different when you were farming for yourself. The chicken coop went up with plenty of room for a couple dozen hens. Jake built it larger than they currently needed so it would meet the future needs of their expanding family. Magnificent the Rooster seemed to know he was ruler over an impressive kingdom. He strutted around, eyeing his concubines, and keeping his princelings in order. The hens were not named. Marina never named anything that might end up in the frying pan or stew pot.

Jake built a fine solid barn with grain bins and a high loft to store the hay. It had shelves for his tools, a work bench where he could repair a chair, a stall for Ol' Jeb and wooden stanchions for two cows. They didn't have the cows yet, but their planning hadn't stopped.

Roy was the first baby born in the new house. It had been three years since she had had an infant. He was such a quiet baby Marina kept checking on him to make sure he was alright. She'd peek in thinking he was asleep and find him watching leaves outside the window, shadows on the wall, or his brother and sisters doing chores nearby. "You're awfully serious for such a tiny thing," she fretted. But like her other children, he was healthy. And so was Emily when she arrived in 1923.

. . .

Marina's days flowed with active joy — caring for the children, working in the garden, canning everything she could find, and farming the cotton fields. *Their* cotton fields, Marina liked to point out. She and Jake still fell into bed drained of their last ounce of energy, but this was a satisfied exhaustion.

The land was well on its way to being cleared. The life they had envisioned from the stoop of a sharecroppers' cabin was being lived out on their front porch — a front porch they owned.

There were setbacks. A family of raccoons killed seven of Marina's best laying hens and all but one of the baby chicks. Blight wiped out most of the cotton during their second harvest. The advantage of home ownership kicked in there. Since they didn't have to give fifty percent of the gross cotton sales to the landowner, they were able to pay for the seed and avoid debt. Thankfully, Marina's garden had done exceptionally well and they had plenty to eat.

Marina spread the whipped egg whites over a lemon pie and popped it back in the oven to brown.

"It's not even Sunday," Jake noted. "What are we celebratin'?"

"Three years on our own land." Marina grinned.

"We can celebrate gettin' a cow too. I'm pickin' her up from Duke Anderson Saturday afternoon."

Surprised, Marina waited for him to explain. "Can we afford to buy a cow?"

"Yes, ma'am. Thanks to land of our own, we're payin' cash."

"I can make my own butter," Marina announced proudly.

August 1925

Baby Hank arrived to a Hartmann farm in full swing. Marina and Jake were busier than they had thought possible, and each child helped in whatever way he or she was able. Rosa Lee assisted with the babies and cooking. Flora and Walt could often be found helping Pappy out in the fields or taking care of the animals. Roy toddled after them with a quiet determination to do his share even if his share meant pulling a handful of weeds. Agreeable Emily traipsed around the house distributing smiles wherever she went.

Marina hummed as she mashed strawberries and lemon juice in her flat-bottomed kettle. As soon as the fruity liquid reached a rolling boil, she dumped sugar in and stirred. Rosa Lee stood beside her, providing hot jelly jars. "Your pappy's going to be pleased to have strawberry jelly on his biscuits tonight at supper.

"Try this, Emily." Marina dabbed a bit of jelly on a biscuit leftover from breakfast.

The little miss smacked her lips. "Mo' p'ease."

Marina laughed. "Too bad strawberries are one berry that doesn't grow wild on our land. Sure was nice of Mrs. Ashabranner to share some of her strawberries with us, wasn't it?" The tiny flaxen-haired head bobbed in agreement.

The kitchen was quiet after dinner until Flora stormed in. "That Walter is too big for his britches!"

Marina handed her ten-year-old daughter a clean cloth. "You dry," she instructed. Nothing helped a young girl sort out life like washing dishes with her mother.

Flora went to work as she continued her tirade. "You should have seen him out in the field! When Pappy's not right there, Walter acts like he's the man of the place. King of the hill! Ha!" Flora placed a dinner dish in the cabinet. "I hope he remembers I'm older than he is, even if he is a boy." She paused. "You know, Mommy, he's always been that way."

"He's always been a boy," Marina reminded her.

Chapter Thirteen

November 1926

Marina laid another egg into the basket, gently cradling it between two others. She shooed a protective Rhode Island Red away from a nesting box. Five more brown eggs. That makes seventeen. Two fewer than yesterday. Could be a cold snap settling in. She better start conserving eggs.

Two baskets firmly in hand, Marina backed out of the chicken coop. Turning around, she noticed Jake, hands on hip, staring at the house. The inscrutable look on his face gave her pause. He was rarely still that long unless he was sleeping. He always had some chore that needed doing. Walking up beside him, she stared at the house, trying to discern what had drawn his attention. "Somethin' wrong?" she finally asked.

"Maybe not." She waited, knowing there were more thoughts to come. He shook his head. "It's been stormin' across the midwest since August. Sioux City is flooded."

"Iowa's a long way from here."

"Not the way the tributaries flow. Every stream leads to the Mississippi, and it's already washin' out bridges and railroads." Jake shook his head again. She waited, giving him time to process the rest of his thoughts. "I believe it would be best if we put the house up on stilts."

Marina glanced in the direction of the river. She understood how fast runoff could reach the Big Lake flood system and if the banks of the Mississippi overflowed. . .or if the unthinkable happened and the levy broke. . . .She nodded agreement.

"We can't start anything new 'til we have the cotton out of the fields. Then I'll get busy on it."

While at the cotton gin two weeks later, several neighboring farmers promised to assist Jake in raising the house. The men knew they could count on him when they needed help. He talked to Clay Burrows, who agreed to lend him two railroad jacks in exchange for a Saturday afternoon of labor. Then he went home to begin the process of preparing the house for lifting. He measured logs and squared them off. When possible, he used trees that had fallen naturally. Next he used a bit and a hammer to drill holes in the beams.

Flora was a great help. She wasn't as tall as her younger brother, but she could match him strength for strength hauling timber. With each child picking up an end, they stacked the beams wherever Pappy directed.

"How'd she get to be so strong?" Jake questioned Marina. "She's not even big-boned."

"That girl's got a strong mind," Marina declared. "When she makes up her mind to do somethin', she just goes ahead and does it. You can't tell her she's not capable."

After two days of preparation, the house was ready to be lifted. Six neighbor men and two of Marina's brothers were at the house shortly after dawn. They laid a pair of timbers parallel under the east and west ends of the house, slipping them through the spaces between the foundation stones. On top of the logs, they laid timbers under the house to provide cribbing. Using an eight-foot handle attached to a railroad jack, they ratcheted the house up six inches on one side, securing it with steel trapping over the beams before ratcheting up the other end and making the house even. Jake checked it with a water level. Next, they inserted shorter beams on top of the corner stones. Then the process of raising the house another six inches was repeated.

The men blew on their hands to ward off the freezing cold. Marina kept the workers supplied with hot coffee by boiling a pot of grounds on the edge of a campfire. To provide them with a hearty stew for their midday meal, she set a heavy iron kettle on top of a makeshift grill of rocks. She also opened a jar of every fruit and vegetable she had canned that summer. The men were satisfied.

Marina and the children watched the progress until the house was an even three feet off the ground on all sides. Then with Walt's enthusiastic help, the men pulled the cribbing out from under the house.

Snow up north continued to melt, racing toward the Mississippi and filling up rivers and streams along her way. Water levels in the Delta continued to rise. One eye on Little River flowing east of their land, Marina moved her hens and an unhappy rooster to the barn loft. The hens clucked in agitation but after a few short flights settled into their new home without much fuss. Magnificent the Rooster, on the other hand, spent the whole day crowing about the loss of his kingdom.

Marina felt satisfied they were safe now that the house had been raised, but Jake continued to look worried. He didn't say much, especially not in front of the children, but he listened intently whenever neighbors shared information about how much rain their relatives in towns up north were getting. After one of those conversations he always rechecked the house, barn, and outbuildings for new cracks or fissures. It seemed to Marina her cautious husband repaired gaps that weren't even there.

And then it began to pour in Mississippi County. The year of 1926 rained itself into history. Warm weather melted the northern snows even faster. January, February, and March of 1927 were measured by how many drops of misery each month contributed to the ever-widening streams, the ever-topping creeks. Some days it was a lonely drizzle; others, a raging storm cracked its whip across the sky. Their land was so close to the wild edges of Big Lake that during particularly violent storms they could hear ancient trees crashing to the ground.

The government with its US Army Corps of Engineers swore the Mississippi River had been tamed. They promised the levies they built from Cairo, Illinois, to New Orleans, Louisiana, would hold. But the massive voice of the storm thundered a message to rich and poor alike. Citizens were not in control, not even the high ranking ones.

"You don't think the levies will fail, do you?" Marina asked, trying to keep the anxiousness she felt out of her voice.

Jake shrugged, not wanting to give his wife the only answer he had. Finally, he admitted, "There's no place for more water to go. Every inch of ground is soaked. The rivers rushin' into the Mississippi are overflowin' before they get there. Billy Clarkson swears the Arkansas River has been runnin' backwards."

"What about the run-offs?"

"They're full too. People like to think of the earth as a giant cistern able to hold whatever the sky pours out, but it's not like that. Once it's saturated, the land won't take any more. Only thing they can do now is reinforce the levies.

"The government may be sayin' the levies are goin' to hold, but I think the engineers are runnin' scared. Word is they've got 30,000 men workin' day and night. The government pulled convicts out of prison to stack sandbags. Negro sharecroppers are being rounded up at gunpoint—forced to stay on top of the levies, not allowed to leave for nothin'. Marina, they're usin' some of those men as human sandbags! It's not just fear of flood either. Landowners are afraid if the Negroes leave, they won't come back and there won't be anybody to do the plantin' in spring." Jake paused. "A few men are sendin' their women and children north. My little sisters would be grown now. If we could find them, maybe you and the kids. . . ."

"No!" Marina responded before his suggestion was complete. "We'll not leave you. We'll not leave our home."

Jake shook his head. "I don't know, Marina. I don't see how anything the engineers are doin' can be enough. Doesn't appear that farmers up north believe it will be either. They aren't wonderin' *if* it's goin' to break. They want to help determine *where* it will break. Folks on both sides of the river know that if the levy breaks on the other side, their own farms will be saved. Police caught men sneakin' over with dynamite aiming to blow holes in the levy and force-flood the land across the river from their own. Both sides are postin' guards now, and from what I hear, the patrols are aimin' to kill."

April arrived. More rain fell. More tension built up. They held their breath, waiting for the inevitable. Everything felt wet. Wood was damp. Laundry never felt completely dry. Food molded faster. To Marina, even her own skin felt clammy.

Then on a gray April morning, the levy ripped apart. The deluge swept away the men working to keep her back. Months of strengthening the levies disappeared in moments, as if the river had only been toying with them before tossing lives and government egos aside. Showing no favoritism, the Mississippi flooded both sides of her boundaries. She was wildly out of control. The "mile-wide river" spread out almost a hundred miles in some flatlands.

Tucked away near Big Lake's eleven thousand acres of sprawling swamp, the Hartmann cabin withstood the storm. Bottomland hardwoods slowed the river's run and soaked up a fair share of water. The wilderness with oak and hickory trees, bushes, flowers, and even grass hindered the flood from affecting their farm as it did the miles of cleared acreage with no vegetation to stop it.

From the doorway of her home, Marina watched swirling, powerful, unrestrained waters. The dancing light so character-istic of the river she knew was nowhere in sight. In its place moved a brown, churning sludge that tossed up glimpses of the storm's plunder. She could see carcasses of pigs and mules careening along with soaked sacks of some family's winter provisions. After glimpsing what appeared to be a man's arm, she turned the children away, refusing to let them watch any-more. But Marina's eyes stayed riveted to the tumultuous sight beyond her windows.

Somewhere up river, the storm's violence had snapped giant trees into helpless logs, floating them along like twigs a child might set down in a creek. One of these knocked into their chicken coop, splintering the shack into scraps before rushing off to damage something else downstream. The smoke house disappeared one night. Flood waters simply swept it off its foundation, taking the intact building along for the ride.

Eventually, the winds quieted. The rains petered out. Like a child throwing a teeth-jarring temper tantrum, the Mississippi River finally exhausted itself.

Chapter Fourteen

April 1927

Marina's house and Jake's barn had withstood the storm. They lost one animal—a cranky old hen that was too stupid to stay up in the loft with the rest of the poultry. She had a tendency to fly at Emily whenever the little girl collected eggs so wasn't considered much of a loss. Before long that bird would have ended up in the stew pot anyway.

The Mississippi River held flood stage for over five months before exhausting her rampage. Brown stolid water, so sluggish it was difficult to believe it had ever possessed power to do damage, sat unmoving on the land.

Most farmers had given up planting a crop that year. Not Jake. Day after day he rowed over his forty acres, monitoring his land. "I think I know how Noah felt when he sent out doves," he commented.

Using a thick hickory limb, Jake measured the water depth. He collected floating garbage to prevent it from lodging in his fields. A few articles of worth floated into his possession. He asked around, attempting to determine rightful owners so the items could be returned. When that wasn't possible, he gave Marina a baking pan and put the elbow for a stove pipe to good use.

Eventually water receded over the river banks, leaving a foot of muck on top of the land. Jake waded through the mud in his work boots, surveying damage, estimating the time it would take to dry out enough to plant.

Marina focused on her garden. She was more worried about planting vegetables than cotton. If they missed a crop, they could survive without most of the items bought by cash. Unlike so many farmers, they bought nothing on credit except their land and essentials they were unable to grow.

Rosa Lee watched the smaller children indoors while Marina and Flora cleared away rocks and as much of the mud and silt as possible. They planted their first attempt at a garden too early, and the seeds drowned in the muck before producing a single shoot. Their second attempt three weeks later mustered a few sprouts that barely lifted a leaf above the silt. The plantings were thin and weak. Then they had a day of rain and most of the plants washed away.

The water finally cleared enough for Jake to plant three quarters of his regular crop. The remaining acreage was still too wet. He pushed the plow through the mud-caked ground and pushed the seed down into its blackness. The result was cotton plants barely twenty-four inches tall when they should have been at least three feet high.

Jake uncharacteristically slumped into his chair. "We've lost most of the crop. We'll barely take enough cotton to gin to pay for the seed."

"Well," Marina reasoned, "we don't need a lot of cash. Our savings in the tobacco box will just about cover the land payments. The girls can wear their dresses another year. Walt is bursting out of his overalls, but I saved an old pair of yours and can make them over for him. Walt's old pair will do fine for Roy. Emily's so little I can make her two dresses out of one flour sack and still have material to cut out a shirt for Hank if I lay the pattern right." Marina nodded to herself, her plan forming as she spoke. "We can do without sugar this year."

"The children," Jake began.

"Those children don't need sugar," she insisted. "It's almost bee season anyway. I noticed a swarm around that old cottonwood tree next to the pump. Walt and Roy can go raid the trunk. I suspect it'll be full of honey." She paused. "We can put off buying that second cow."

Encouraged, Jake stood up. "You're right. All this flooding will prepare the land for a good crop next year." He smiled. "We have a stack of old boards stored in the barn. I believe

I'll pull out and straighten the nails so I can build you a new smokehouse."

Busy in the fields, Jake had no idea how Marina agonized over her vegetables. Regardless of the cotton crop, they had always had enough food on their table. She knew if the garden failed now, not only would their summer produce be gone, but also everything she would have preserved for winter. Without a word to the family, she began conserving canned items she had remaining from last season.

In that fall of 1927 Marina checked on her beans and tomatoes almost as often as she did her children. She combed the woods, searching for greens, mushrooms, nuts, wild rhubarb, and anything else she could cook or preserve. She willed her garden to grow, and it did. Peppers and cucumbers did especially well in the moist soil.

Marina was stuffing peppers for dinner when a thump made her wonder if the door was flying off its hinges. Hank and Roy barreled through, shouting, "We're done! We're done! The new barn fence is finished!"

Roy added. "Every nail's in place. There ain't a tornado nor flood that could tear it down now. We built it strong."

Jake and Walt followed with grins almost as big. "It appears solid." Jake agreed.

"That's fine!" Delighted, Marina congratulated her men. "Give me a minute to stick these peppers in the oven and I'll come see it. Flora, grab the slop bowl and toss the vegetable leavings to the hens."

"I helped with the fence too, Mommy," Hank claimed.

"You did not," an indignant Roy contradicted.

"Yep, I did," Hank insisted calmly.

"What did you do?" Roy challenged.

"I told you that you were doing it right."

They all laughed and Jake tousled the two-year-old's head. "I guess you were the foreman."

Pleased to have his contribution recognized, Hank nodded.

"Well then, Mr. Foreman, come help me put Ol' Jeb in his stall," Walt ordered. "I'm wonderin' if you could show me how to feed him while we're out there. I seem to have forgotten, but I'll watch you real good and maybe I'll learn how." The two raced out the screen door. Still laughing, the rest of the family followed.

Perseverance paid off. They ate chicken and dumplin's almost every night, and frankly it was more dumplin' than chicken, but nobody went hungry and they made it through the winter.

. . .

February 1928 arrived. Jake was in the fields once again and Marina was pleased to put out onion sets. Inpatient to see her garden, she planted the moment a new moon appeared. Spring was kind and soon green shoots shot through that beautiful Arkansas soil. Their farm was finally getting back to normal after the flood.

They were in the middle of supper when Marina announced her news. "Dr. Franklin says I'm having twins."

The children cheered. Jake got up from his chair, leaving his half-finished plate sitting there. Without a word or expression, he started for the door.

"Where are you goin'?" Marina called.

"Out to the barn" he answered over his shoulder. "If we're goin' to have a family of ten, I'd better get started buildin' a bigger dinner table."

. . .

Sadie and Samuel were different as fire and water. Sammy had the red hair but was a peaceful, smiling little guy. Sadie, on the other hand, was a black-haired little minx who arrived speaking her mind. Marina had been worried about having more children, especially after such a difficult year on the farm. Now that she had them, she was thankful she hadn't had a choice.

A month later, their cow, Buttermilk, gave birth to twin calves. They named one Buttercup and sold the unnamed calf for cash to pay on their land mortgage. Each morning, Walt opened the gate to let Buttermilk and Buttercup graze in the woods. Every evening the cows would meander their way back.

If they wandered too long, he and Flora followed the sound of their bells, leading them home in time for milking.

. . .

Jake continued making improvements on their land. They'd lived there enough years that it no longer felt new. It just felt like home and that was even better.

Rosa Lee, Flora, Emily, and Hank rummaged the woods looking for wild blackberry vines to raid. The girls had strict instructions to eat a few but pick the majority for preserves. Hank didn't care anything about the future. He wanted to stuff his mouth with the plump, sun-warmed berries as fast as possible. After a couple encounters with thorns though, he plopped down on his little bottom, crying for the berries to come to him. Rosa Lee laughed at the sight of his cross expression in a purple-blue-stained face. Then she pacified him with her choicest picks.

. . .

1929's hot summer melted into a fruitful harvest for the Hartmann family. Unfortunately, not everyone in the community was doing so well. The stock market crashed in October. Banks and stores quit giving credit so liberally. Many of the families they knew were devastated. Desperate for cash, one of their neighbors gave up farming and determined to look for factory work up north. The man offered to sell his mule dirt cheap. Jake, who needed a second mule, refused. "I'll buy your mule 'cause he's a good one, but I'll pay full price. I won't cheat a man 'cause he's down," Jake told him.

They sat on the porch after supper. Flora knelt beside her mother's rocker so she could get close. "Mommy, pickin' season's almost over," she began softly. Marina was surprised by the girl's hesitant, almost apprehensive tone. "Soon the school term will be startin' up again. I was wonderin' if I could go."

Puzzled, Jake looked over at the two of them. "You graduated eighth grade, Flora. That's as high as Blackwater School goes."

"That's true, Pappy." She glanced nervously at her mother, who then took up the conversation.

"Flora has always done so well in school that the teacher invited her to come back for one more year. Miss Tindle told Flora she could use her books to keep studyin'."

"What about you?" Jake asked Marina. "You were lookin' forward to the extra help at home."

Marina looked at Flora's anxious face. The girl loved to learn. She was always scribbling math problems on any scrap she could find. And when she couldn't find any paper, Flora grabbed a long stick and worked out her calculations in the dirt. "I'll manage," she answered.

Jake nodded. "If your mother thinks she can spare you, then it's alright with me. You can go."

Flora jumped up, whooping and hollering. "Thank you," she shouted and raced off the porch to share the good news with Rosa Lee.

Her parents watched her go, wondering at the girl's natural love for school. "I never had much formal schoolin'," Jake commented, "just a year or two. I'd like our children to get whatever education they're inclined to."

Marina nodded. "It'd be nice if their lives were a little bit easier than ours have been."

"They will be," Jake assured her. "We started from nothin' as sharecroppers. Our children are landowners!" Jake's grin and pride were both as wide as the day they had bought their property. He was right. Their children's lives would be easier.

Chapter Fifteen

July 1930

Marina stood at her kitchen counter, worry lines showing on her forehead. The sun wasn't up and neither were the children. She and Jake had a rare opportunity to talk without being interrupted. Picking up the coffee pot, she crossed the kitchen to where her husband sat by himself at the head of the table. She poured them both a cup before returning the pot to the stove.

"The list in the paper of people who are delinquent on their taxes is getting longer every week," she commented, sitting down beside him. "What does the government do? They raise the taxes even higher. It doesn't make sense. They say the country's in a depression. Everybody has less money. How can the answer be to raise taxes?"

Jake nodded, his face full of compassion for neighbors losing their homes. "The government is trying to prevent another flood like the one we had three years ago. The increased taxes are supposed to pay for a new drainage system in the county."

"We won't need a new system if nobody can afford to live here," Marina protested.

Jake smiled, then turned serious again. "It's not just the taxes. Before the flood, people weren't payin' cash for anything. They put everything on credit. They borrowed money, takin' a chance they'd be able to pay it back, and now," he turned his hands up in a helpless gesture, "now they can't." Jake shook his head. "That's just foolishness to use credit like that. It catches up with people." Switching the subject, he informed her, "The boys and I are going to build a pig pen out at the barn today."

"Do you have enough wire?"

He nodded. "I bought wire from Bart Angleson. He and his wife have given up farmin' and moved to Detroit for factory work. Even at a fair price, I hate to buy part of a farm that's being broken up, but they need the money. Bart said he'd rather think part of his farm was goin' on here than to know it was just deserted. And he surely didn't want to leave the bank any more than he had to."

"Did the bank really have to foreclose on him? They won't be able to sell the house anyway. Too many others are for sale. Couldn't they have given him some extra time?" Marina asked.

"Bank gave him six months. I don't know that any more would have made any difference. The Scofields over on Right Hand Stumpy Road deserted their house in the middle of the night. Just took off and left it. Nobody knows where they've gone, or if they do, they're not sayin'."

Even though the children were asleep, Marina whispered. "But so many people are losing their homes. *We* won't lose our land, will we, Jake?"

"No, we won't, Marina. Cotton prices are hittin' bottom. We won't get much per bale, but it'll be enough. We've never missed a payment on the land yet and we never will. The added taxes will be tough, but we can make it. We just need to cut back on things a little bit."

Marina sipped her coffee. She wondered where they could cut but didn't say anything. No use being negative. Besides, Jake was right. They'd make it work even if they had to eat vinegar dumplin's every day.

Later that evening Marina and the girls were clearing the supper table. She picked up a dish, raking the leftovers off into the slop bucket.

"Mommy," Flora asked for Marina's attention. "Rosa Lee and I were thinking it would be easier on you if instead of havin' to make our dresses for the school recitation, we bought them this year."

Marina stopped scrubbing the table to focus. "Bought them?" she repeated.

"Yes, Tiger-Levine's has some nice dresses."

"Some of the dresses even have lace around the collar," Rosa Lee added.

Marina resumed scrubbing the table. "I'm sure they do. And when you're grown and you and your husband have a farm of your own, I'll be proud to see you wear all your dresses with lace and know you bought them uptown at Tiger-Levine's. Now make sure you dry those glasses well so they don't streak."

Unwilling to let the discussion die, Flora tried again. "We like the dresses you make, but you're so busy. Buyin' our dresses would save you the trouble of havin' to make them. Amy and Lynette Cox's mother buys all their dresses straight off the rack at Tiger-Levine's."

"Yes, and she puts ever' one of them on credit too." Marina increased her scrubbing of the table with a force that looked as if her goal was to shave the grain right off.

"Pappy buys all our farmin' supplies on credit," Flora pushed.

"Farmin' supplies, yes! We have to buy seed and flour, things we can't grow on the farm or do without. But your father pays them off every harvest. The Coxes carry their debt from one year to the next. That's like livin' your life on charity. I'll be glad when the day comes that we don't have to put a thing on credit. But until it does, we won't put one penny more than we have to on it. Now take that slop bucket out to the chickens. I don't want to hear another word about it."

"Yes, ma'am." The girls knew when their mother was immovable.

Alone in the kitchen, Marina let out a long, aggravated sigh. Why on earth were the girls putting her in a position where she had to tell them no. She hung up her wet dishcloth and retreated to the bedroom. She had intended to cut out pieces for the girls' dresses tonight. Now she felt like flinging the cloth out the window. She understood her daughters wanting to select their dresses, to choose between yellow and pink, to have eyelet instead of cotton, to wear a dress from a catalogue instead of something she had cut out of flour sack. Tired, she sat down on the end of the feather bed. "They ought to wear beautiful dresses," she complained to herself.

Sighing, she pulled the flour sacks out from storage under her bed and examined them critically. At least the flower print looked summery. She didn't have any lace, but she could trim the cuffs with scraps of white cotton. Maybe she could find enough solid pink and yellow quilt scraps to sew them each a hair bow. Marina nodded to herself. She'd make it work. Suddenly she realized she was sitting on the feather bed, an offense she would have swatted her children for committing.

On Saturday, Jake took his plowing tools in to be sharpened while Marina shopped Tiger-Levines' General Store. She was greeted by a pleasant-looking young man with soft brown hair.

"Good-afternoon, Miz Hartmann. Ever'body in your family doin' alright?"

"Yes, they are, Mr. Borowski. Thank you for askin'. How are you and your brother doin'?"

"Fine, thank you. What can I do for you?"

"I'll take a pound of coffee, a spool of your dark blue thread, a dozen black buttons, and a yard of cheesecloth."

"Fine," he approved. "Anything else?"

"I believe that's everything."

"I'll have it ready for you in a few minutes."

"Thank you." Marina wandered through the store. She had stopped in front of the ribbons when the door opened and Polly Patrice Cox promenaded in. She wished there was a way to avoid the woman, but the long skinny aisles of the general store didn't offer much hope. She inched toward the end of the aisle just as a shrill voice reached her.

"Hello, Marina."

"Polly Patrice." Marina greeted her with more civility than warmth.

"So nice to see you in from the country again! Poor thing! I don't know how you stand it, trapped out there. I love livin' in town where ever'thin' happens."

"Oh, quite a bit happens out on our farm too."

"I see that it does. Here you are expectin' *again*."

Marina flushed and met this comment with a stony smile. She hoped the woman would drop the subject, but the Polly Patrices of this world are not stopped by good-mannered hints. She prattled on. "That woman from the hills, Pearl McDowell, she lives out by you too, doesn't she?"

"About three-quarters of a mile."

146

"She's expectin' again too. I've noticed ever' time she has a baby, you just run to catch up with her. How many children will this one make now?"

"Nine," Marina replied, tersely turning away from the woman to examine ribbon choices. Good-manners could fly out the window. She was done with this discussion.

Polly Patrice's eyes followed Marina's. "Oh, are you lookin' at ribbons?"

Marina practically grunted the necessary affirmation.

In a sugar-sweet voice that could drown a rat, Polly Patrice cooed, "My, my. I can't wait to see how you take yet another old flour sack and turn it into a beautiful, homespun dress. I sure couldn't do it. I just buy my girls ready-made dresses from here at the store."

Marina's insides stiffened, She felt livid with Polly Patrice and angry with herself for allowing someone she didn't even like to make her feel inferior. She looked down the aisle towards the counter. "Mr. Borkowski, is my order ready?"

"Yes, ma'am. I didn't want to interrupt your conversation with Mrs. Cox."

Marina paid him in cash and murmured goodbye to both. She grabbed her bundles up with such relief that Mr. Borkowski chided himself for not noticing Mrs. Hartmann was in a rush this afternoon.

Marina sat silent most of the drive home. After seventeen years of marriage, Jake understood there were times to ask your wife if she was alright and other times to wait and see what happened. This was a wait and see time.

That evening after the children were sleeping, they retired to their room. Voice strained with a failed attempt to sound casual, Marina remarked, "I believe I'll sell a couple of the hens to buy Rosa Lee and Flora dresses from Tiger-Levine's to wear to the school recitation."

Jake's eyes traveled to the trunk at the end of the bed where two lengths of flour sack lay washed, pressed and ready to be made into dresses. He looked back at his wife standing there. He didn't understand what was happening, but he knew it meant much more than dresses to her. "That sounds like a fine idea, Marina."

School Recitation Day arrived. Marina's heart filled with pride as she reviewed her children. Rosa Lee and Flora radiated confidence in their first store-bought dresses. White lace edged the sleeves and neckline of Rosa Lee's dress. The blue print matched her eyes perfectly. Flora's puffed sleeved were scalloped to match her neckline. A thin belt emphasized her slender waist. Walt, Roy, Hank, and Sammy were scrubbed clean and handsome as their daddy. Emily and Sadie primped in the pretty dresses she had made them out of their sisters' discarded flour prints.

A movement caught her eye and she saw Hank pull a tiny frog from his pocket. He sneaked a quick glance to see if she had noticed. She had and gave him "the look." Disappointed, but not quelled, Hank slipped the little critter back into his pocket.

After the recitation ended, Polly Patrice made a beeline for the exiting Hartmanns. "Oh, Marina," she oozed, "I see Rosa Lee and Flora *finally* got store-bought dresses."

"Yes," Marina replied with even more sweetness than Polly Patrice herself could muster, "and I didn't buy them on credit neither."

Chapter Sixteen

September 1930

Lilli arrived with the harvest. "She's a little bitty thing," Jake commented. Marina was too tired to respond, but when she looked down at the baby, she knew another crystal moment of joy.

The next six weeks tumbled into each other. Cucumbers needed to be pickled, corn dried, tomatoes canned. The children helped her bank potatoes and apples in dirt mounds for winter. It seemed like the work would never be done, but Marina enjoyed her tasks and took pride in the bright, clear color of her canned peaches.

"Mornin'," a male voice called out. The door swung open and heavy footsteps entered the house without waiting for a response. The sound startled Marina. Rosa Lee and Flora had taken the younger children over to the river to catch frogs. Other than Lilli, she was alone in the house.

She swung around from the cook stove where she was frying potatoes in time to see Eddie slump into Jake's chair at the head of the table. "Thought I'd drop by for a cup of coffee and a conversation with Jake. He around?"

"No." Still shaken, she refrained from pointing out that her husband was where every decent man was at 10:30 in the morning — in the field. She hesitated. Maybe if she didn't offer the coffee, he would decide not to wait.

"Well, that's alright, I'll just wait around for him. Where's that cup of coffee you were talkin' 'bout?"

Marina opened the cupboard and took out the mug she had just finished washing and drying. But I'll be danged if I'm gonna cut into that blackberry pie, she fumed to herself.

As if he could read her mind and smell the blackberries through the pie safe, Eddie remarked, "This coffee sure hits the spot. The only thing that would make it taste better would be a big old piece of your blackberry pie. . . ." His words trailed off as if waiting for her to finish his thoughts. Marina smiled, but offered nothing.

"Or maybe a slab of apple pie. . . ."

He's fishin,' she realized with satisfaction. He doesn't know what I have in the pie safe. He's just hopin' there's something sweet in there. Well, he can hope all he wants. No one's touching that pie until Sunday dinner. She picked up the coffee pot. "Here, Eddie. Why don't you finish off the rest of this coffee you like so well."

Disappointed, he sighed and looked around for something else to distract him. His eyes lit outside the window and settled on the wooden door to the root cellar. He sat up straight, his eyes gleaming. "Marina, you know what I'd like to do? I'd like to take Momma a jar of your kraut. You know how she just loves your sauerkraut—says nobody can make it like you do. Would you mind if I took a jar home to her?"

Marina didn't recall Aunt Dolce ever commenting on her sauerkraut before, but she couldn't think of a way to politely refuse Eddie either.

"Do you mind gettin' it now so's I won't forget?" Eddie pushed.

Marina set down her spatula and turned off the fire under the potatoes. "I'll be just a moment, Eddie," she promised. Maybe if she gave him the sauerkraut, he'd leave faster. She walked outside, opened the cellar door, took down the steps, and selected a nice jar of kraut. She couldn't have been gone more than a few minutes. When she returned, Eddie was nowhere in sight. "Eddie," she called.

No answer.

"If that don't beat all," she muttered to herself. She turned to go put the jar of kraut back in the cellar when a scraping noise caught her attention. Marina crossed the plank floor to the bedroom. Peering past the curtain doorway, she saw Eddie down on his knees beside their bed, pushing their Luxor cigar box back under the bed frame.

152

She watched as he struggled to his feet. What on earth could he be doing? He must think we keep money under there. Well, Marina thought with satisfaction, this is one time I'm proud we haven't got an extra dollar to our name. We just made the land payment yesterday. The only things in that cigar box are receipts for the monthly mortgage payments on our land, and they won't do him a lick of good.

She spoke before he saw her, "Did you lose somethin'?"

The sound of her voice startled him. He whirled around and began chattering like a jabbering bird. "No, no, I mean yes. Yes, I did."

"What did you lose? I'll help you look for it," Marina baited him.

"I lost a. . .a. . . ." He stared down at his hands for inspiration and found it in the fiddling with his jacket. He seized on the answer as if it had been supplied from heaven. "A button. Yes! I lost a button. It just popped right off while I was drinkin' coffee." His eyes traced the distance from the table where he had been sitting in the kitchen to where he stood now. "And it rolled. It rolled, and it rolled all the way over here." He smiled triumphantly.

Marina looked down at her spotless floor. "I'll get the broom and help you look," she offered. "Let me see one of the others so I'll know what it looks like."

"No, no. That's not necessary." Eddie pulled the jacket tight around him. "Momma's got another one at home. I don't 'spect

153

we'll ever find the one I lost. No, it's long gone. It really rolled." He began backing toward the door. "I'll not wait any longer on Jake. I'll jist get on home and see him another time."

"Here's a quart of sauerkraut for Aunt Dolce." Marina held out the jar to her meddlesome cousin.

Still clutching his jacket, he took two steps toward her, grabbed the quart jar, and fled out the front door. Marina stood there watching for a moment, then began to laugh. "I sure am glad he's one of a kind."

She checked in on baby Lilli. Her newborn was sleeping peacefully. It would be another hour before she would wake up, wanting to be fed.

Five more minutes and the potatoes were close to being done. Marina turned off the fire underneath them. She'd finish them up right before Jake and the older children came in from the field so they'd be hot and fresh. Picking up a wet wash rag, she began to wipe the table where Eddie had sat.

Next, moving swiftly because she wanted time with her flowers, she picked tomatoes, onions, beans, carrots, zucchini, celery, and potatoes. Back in the house, she tossed pepper into the almost-ready chicken stock and began to slice the vegetables. Peel, slice, chop. She had repeated those same actions so many times her knife flew as if it had a mind of its own. She used the time to plan. Lily-of the-valley and other spring bulbs needed to be planted. Peonies needed to be divided. Rose bushes were ready to be pruned back. She wouldn't get to it all today, but she'd get done what she could.

She tossed the soup makings into the pot, wiped her hands, and grabbed pruning shears.

Marina couldn't resist peeking in on Lilli again. She held her breath, afraid Lilli would sense her presence and wake up, crying to be fed. Her luck held. The infant slept sweetly on. One ear tuned for her baby's cry, she stepped outside.

Marina appreciated her vegetable garden, but she cherished her flowers. Their beauty soaked into the core of her soul. From spring until late fall a wide swath of blooms guided the path to the door and encircled their home. Tall deep-scarlet hollyhocks, showy yellow zinnias, and sprays of roses camouflaged the empty space between the ground and the bottom of the cabin. At different times through the seasons, the scent of purple hyacinths, giant snowball bushes, bridal wreaths, and several sizes of sunflowers perfumed her yard.

Since the planting did not have to be uprooted every three to four years, they could now spread out and multiply. Whenever she noticed a grouping of flowers dying out in the center or flopping over, Marina divided and planted again. Jake joked that her goal was to replant all the cotton fields with flowers. She teased back that if he stood still too long, she might plant a flower on him. Marina couldn't argue the point too much though. She had cultivated sweet-smelling honeysuckle vines around the outhouse and even planted bright poppies around hollowed-out trees to attract bees.

Some of the plants she grew were native to Big Lake. Others she had ordered from the Sears catalogue over the years. The profusion of flowers and colors gave her yard a feeling of abundance.

Marina relished every aspect of flower gardening. In winter, she looked over seed catalogues, deciding what to select. Rarely had there been a year she couldn't order at least one new plant. In spring, she couldn't wait to get her hands into the dirt. It thrilled her to see strong green shoots pushing up. Marina fancied the flowers talked to her. It tickled her to see how they'd quiver all over and stand a little taller when she gave them a long, cool drink of water. She didn't even mind pumping gallons of water. In fact, if a day had been particularly demanding or frustrating, she found it therapeutic to pump that handle hard until water gushed out.

Marina took a deep breath. She knew exactly how much sun every foot of land around her house received. She knew which flowers needed to be tucked among bigger plants for shade and which could handle ten hours of Arkansas sun. Working clockwise around the house, she began to snip. Marina cut back her rose bushes and vines. She deadheaded marigolds, coneflowers, and black-eyed Susans, scattering any seeds she didn't need among the plants. Sometimes they took root on their own. Soon, she lost herself in her work.

In a few weeks it would be time to cut the rest of the bushes back. That always felt a little sad. Probably the memory of all the years spent sharecropping. Every third year she had to cut back plants she wouldn't see again. Marina always left a few bulbs, vines, and flowering perennials for the next family although it irritated her to pass by and see someone had torn them out and planted cotton up to the stoop. People like that ought to be shot, she muttered to herself.

Marina stripped a few leaves off the poppies in hopes more of their energy would go into making blooms. Arkansas soil was almost too fertile to grow poppies.

"Now when our children get married, I'll give them starts from my garden, and they'll know how to take care of them," she informed the roses. She had almost worked her way around to the south side of the house when Lilli woke up.

Cuddling a satisfied baby close, she stole a moment to sit on the front porch. A cool breeze was flowing. The fragrance of honeysuckle floated up, sweetening the mood even more. In the distance, Marina could see Rosa Lee, Flora, Emily, Hank, Sadie, and Samuel traipsing across the field. They were coming home to Hartmann land.

Chapter Seventeen

November 1930

T he day Jake took his last load of cotton to the gin, Marina made a peach cobbler for dessert. The fruit had ripened perfectly. Butter gently browned the crust, giving it an almost caramelized taste. An extra dash of salt across the top perfected the pastry. Marina was quite pleased with herself.

It was a rare, lazy evening, one in which the family could draw a sigh of relief at another successful harvest. Autumn chill prevented them from sitting out on the porch, but they were content with the woodstove warming the house comfortably. Jake was perusing a farmer's catalogue, already planning for next season. Rosa Lee, now sixteen, entertained Lilli and dreamed about a boy named Mac she had met at a church social. Flora was devouring a book she had borrowed from a friend up the road. Walt and Roy had a game of checkers going. Much to his delight, the younger brother was winning. Emily, her hands always busy, was cutting out a dress pattern for baby Lilli. Hank alternated between annoying the chess game and bossing the twins, who were making up their own game. Everyone was relaxed, and Marina planned to join them as soon as she put these last dishes away.

Jake answered a knock at the door. The shadowy figures of two men in suits stood there on the other side of the screen door. "Evenin', gentlemen," Jake greeted them. "How can I help you?"

The older of the two men answered. "We're looking for the home of Jacob Hartmann. Would that be you?"

"It would. Come on in."

The dark figures stepped through the screen door where Marina was able to get a better look at them. The shorter man moved with confidence, indicating he was the one in charge. "I'm Arthur Pence." He appeared to be about fifty years of age. His slick black hair was combed away from his face. "This is my associate, Eugene Tobler." Marina guessed the taller man to be much younger, maybe twenty-four. He was lanky and moved around a lot as though he had stopped growing last week and wasn't yet comfortable with the length of his limbs.

"Mr. Pence. Mr. Tobler, have a seat, please," Jake invited them.

The children sat up straight as soon as the men entered. All idle comments ceased. Had they been outside, the children would have scattered, knowing men in suits meant adult

159

business. Inside there was nowhere else for them to go, so they did their best to make themselves invisible.

The men looked around, appraising the house. "Nice place," Mr. Tobler commented.

"Thank you," Jake answered. "We like it." Marina smiled. Her husband's pride in ownership was obvious even when he was trying to be humble.

Marina headed back to the kitchen to make coffee. Rosa Lee immediately handed Lilli off to Flora and went to assist her mother. By the time coffee was ready, she had scooped up large helpings of peach cobbler, topping them off with fresh cream. The men were still making small talk when refreshments were served. They looked rather surprised by the hospitality but responded courteously. Eugene Tobler took one bite and exclaimed, "This is the best peach cobbler I've ever tasted in my life."

The older man frowned at his associate, but then smiled and agreed.

Jake waited until they had finished eating before asking, "How can I help you, gentlemen?"

"Well, sir, we're from the Raizon Title Company. We've come about your house contract."

The men paused, but Jake simply waited for them to go on.

"We know times are tough. Lots of people are havin' trouble makin' their payments."

Jake nodded and spread his hands in a questioning gesture. "That's true. Have you come about one of our neighbors? Are you collectin' to help someone?"

The two men looked at each other, then down at the floor. Marina began to get an uneasy feeling. Something wasn't right here.

"No, sir," Mr. Pence answered slowly. "We've come about you. The company has decided to repossess our property."

"Your property? This is my property. I built this house with my own two hands. That's my barn out there with my animals in it."

"True, you built the house and barn, and I believe there are a couple other outbuildings. But sir, you did it with wood cut from our trees grown right here on our land."

"Yes, and I'm payin' for it monthly. I have a contract."

"That's right," Mr. Tobler joined in. "You have a contract, and the contract states that payments must be made by the first of each month. According to our records, you haven't made a payment in eight months."

"Your records are mistaken. You must've confused ours with another property. We've never been late even one day." He looked toward his wife. "Marina?"

She was already on her way to their bedroom. She pulled out the cigar box where they kept the land receipts. Without opening it, she hurried back handing it over to Jake.

"These are our receipts for every month for the past nine years. We have a fifteen-year contract." Jake opened the box and handed over the receipts wrapped with a rubber band. Marina noticed they were not bound as neatly as she kept them and wondered if Hank had gotten into them.

A couple minutes passed while the men reviewed the receipts. Mr. Pence spoke first. "I see here that you were making all your payments right on time until the last eight months. It's been hard on a lot of folks since the flood."

"We didn't miss any payments — not even after the flood. Yes, we lost our crop, but I cut more trees. We made every payment."

Mr. Tobler handed the stack of receipts back to him. "There are no receipts here for the past eight months," he announced.

"We always put them here." Jake looked through the receipts. He looked up at Marina. "They're gone."

"Eddie took them."

"What?"

"My cousin Eddie was here a couple of weeks ago. He asked for you, but it was midmornin'. You were out in the field. At first, he said he would wait. I was afraid he'd be here all day. Then he asked for a jar of sauerkraut for Aunt Dolce. I went out to the cellar to get it, and when I came back, he was on the floor lookin' at somethin' under the bed. I didn't say anything to you afterwards because I thought he was lookin' for money, and I knew there wasn't any in the cigar box."

Marina and Jake turned to face at the two men representing Raizon Title Company.

Mr. Pence acted as if he hadn't heard the conversation between Marina and Jake. "Our records show you have not made a payment in eight months. If you don't have additional receipts, then we will have to assume our records are correct. Please have everything that belongs to you packed up and off the property by the first of the month."

Jake stood. "It's time for you gentlemen to leave."

They sent the children to bed and went outside to the dying twilight where they could talk in private. The air was cold and Marina shivered. She could already feel winter closing in on them. "Can the title company really make us leave our home?"

"They can if we don't have proof we've paid," Jake answered grimly.

"We'll get the receipts back from Eddie. He doesn't need them. He probably just grabbed them by accident when he was searchin' for money."

"Honey, he wasn't searchin' for money. He was after those eight months of receipts. Eddie's in on it with the company."

Marina shook her head not wanting to believe her cousin could do something so horrendous to her family.

"Think about it," Jake continued. "The company claims to have no record for the exact months that we are missin' receipts. The company men came now — a couple weeks after Eddie stole them, but before our next payment is due."

"Get the receipts back! Go see him tomorrow and demand he give them to us."

Jake nodded. "I'll go tomorrow, but my guess is the receipts have already been destroyed. I don't think the company would have sent their men out here if they hadn't felt sure they were safe from discovery."

Jake was out of the house early the next morning and back before the children had finished breakfast. She could tell from the look on his face that the news was not good but waited until the children were off doing chores before asking.

"Eddie's gone. According to your Aunt Dolce, he left on a train for Chicago yesterday morning. She says he has a new job and went for trainin'."

"A new job?"

"Yep." Jake's face looked gray. "He's working for the Raizon Title Company."

Marina turned away, staring out the window.

"What I don't know is, why us?" Jake continued. "They can't do this to everyone, or they'd be found out. Why did they pick us?"

Her back still to him, Marina pointed outside. "That's why. Look at that barn. How much do you think it's worth? Look at this house. With all the improvements you've added, how much do you think they can sell it for? Do you know anyone else in this entire area who has increased the value of his property so much in this amount of time?"

Jake looked around at the home he had built, the barn, the smokehouse. Nine years, a labor of love for the family he adored, and now he had nothing. It was all gone. He looked more worn out than he had when he spent sixteen hours a day building.

Out the window she could see the twins tagging after Hank and Emily. The sight of her children jerked Marina into a protective stance. "So what will we do?" she asked.

"We pack up and go," Jake answered.

"Go where?" Fear made her voice rise in pitch.

Jake looked down and shook his head. "Go back to being sharecroppers. We don't have any other options. I'll go talk to Clay."

He started to turn away, but she stopped him. "What will we tell the children?"

"The Truth! We'll tell them that we paid every penny right on time and that sometimes that's not enough."

Fighting back tears, Marina began packing that afternoon. Jake said there was no point in putting it off. Delay would only make it more painful. Marina wondered how it could possibly be more painful. As she had suspected, the hardest part was telling the children. They were looking for an answer. They wanted justice. Their parents could give them neither.

By the end of the third day, packing was complete. It took several trips to get their household belongings and the animals over to the green sharecroppers' bungalow where they would be living on Clay's land.

"The children can help you dig up your plants," Jake suggested.

Marina refused. "I said that was the last time I would move those plants, and I meant it. I'll not move them again."

Chapter Eighteen

December 1930

Marina heard through her mother that Eddie was back in town. Neighbors confirmed he had a job with the Raizon Title Company. Marina had never felt such utter loathing for anyone. She felt powerless against the stranglehold this hatred had on her heart, and she felt guilty that it was a member of her family who had been the source of this harm.

"He was the bootlicker in the title company's game." Jake reasoned, hoping to lessen his wife's guilt. "If he hadn't stolen the receipts, they would have paid somebody else to do it."

"If he hadn't been family, we wouldn't have been so vulnerable, and they never would have gotten hold of the receipts."

Winter had come again. The weather ought to have been a sharp cold to match the pain in her heart or at least a heavy white snow that could pretend to cover her misery. Instead, the frost was mild, almost as though it was laughing at her or discounting the wrong that had been done.

The guilt was consuming her. She ought to have known. She ought to have suspected he was up to no good. Even when they were children, she hadn't trusted him. So why did she leave him alone in the house? She could have waited to give him the sauerkraut as he was leaving. If only she had insisted he show her what was under his coat. She had thought he was trying to cover up the fact that there weren't any buttons missing. If only she hadn't assumed she knew his motive.

The pain was immense, her anguish pushing her to a place not even Jake could reach. It distanced her from her children. She wanted to help them, and Jake, heal from their own grief. They were suffering too. Most of their children didn't remember having ever lived anywhere else. The youngest six had been born here. But trapped in her own grief, Marina had nothing to give.

She confided in her mother. Hattie advised Marina to fight against her pain by working even harder. Marina nodded, appreciating the wisdom with which the words were given. If anyone understood deep sorrow, it was Hattie. Marina couldn't imagine what it must have been like to be so young and alone with no financial or emotional support, three lonely children who missed their papa, and another baby due in two months. Even after Hattie moved her family closer to town, other than living on family land, the responsibility was all her own.

Marina knew her loss didn't compare to what her mother had gone through. She tried to follow Hattie's advice, but her identity was wrapped up in this dream of a home of their own. Marina worked hard, never shirking her duties as a wife and mother. If anything, she worked harder, longer hours. But the joy of service was gone.

All through the dark season, Marina was glad she had left her plants and flowers behind. Flowers around the cabin had represented the beauty in her life and faith in their future. Now they were no longer landowners. They were sharecroppers again, buying the seed, doing the work, and giving half the profit to someone else. Land-grubbers. Where was the joy in that!

Clay Burrows assigned them an untouched forty. It had to be cleared before anything could be planted. Walt was now strong enough to swing a steady axe alongside Jake. Roy faithfully tended the fires required to burn out the giant stumps.

March 1931

Spring came even though Marina wasn't looking for the resurrection. Still lost in a gray world, she could see the shades of green, the rosy tinge of a rising sun, and the primitive burst of color as it set, but the beauty no longer touched her heart.

Gardening, which Marina had always found to be a peaceful way to spend an afternoon, was simply another hurdle to overcome. Space for the sun to shine and the vegetables to grow had to be carved out of the woods. She planted her usual-sized vegetable plot, but no flowers, not even marigolds to keep mosquitoes away. "Let them come," she muttered to herself.

As sharecroppers, they did all the same work they had done on their own farm. Landowners were paid their fifty percent first. Out of the remaining money, sharecroppers paid all the bills. Then, if anything was left, it was theirs.

In their previous homes, Marina had always insisted on surrounding her family with wide swaths of zinnias, intermingling the reds, yellows, and purples. Her trailing rose vines had curled their way around posts on the front porch, and in fall brilliant marigolds lit the pathway home. She didn't request it, but Jake silently left bare space for the flowers, a prayer of sorts for his wife's broken heart.

Flora worked behind the mules, plowing the fields. Her mental and physical strength was a gift to the family. They needed her and she didn't seem to mind, but oh, how Marina hated seeing her girl out there. This wasn't the life Marina had imagined for her smart daughter with the extra schooling and a heart for learning.

Mild weather allowed for early planting. Marina and the girls put on sunbonnets and headed for the fields to join Jake and the older boys.

Marina kept an eye on Hank, Sadie, Samuel, and Lilli as she chopped weeds. Whacking away, she mentally worked the math, figuring out how much cotton they would need to bale before breaking even. Marina stopped working for a moment to do a headcount. They were all there, dirt smeared across their faces, arms, and legs. "This is a fine heritage we're giving our children," she muttered.

Jake noticed her movement and looked over to smile. She pretended not to notice and continued her work.

Feelings of guilt increased her bitterness and self-loathing. Jake was a good man. He deserved a cheerful wife. She knew she had so much to be grateful for. The kids were all healthy. They had a roof over their heads and food on the table. She should be happy. She often told herself to be. But the dark cloud was too heavy to lift.

Gradually the sting and regret of losing their home gave way to a general crabbiness with the whole family. Depression settled over her heart, and, as is the way of all bitterness, eventually invaded the sacred haven reserved for Jake and the children. She found herself impatient and short-tempered.

"Flora, go out and milk that cow," Marina snapped. "I can't do everything around here by myself. You children need to help."

Startled, Flora put her pencil down. Leaving her book on the table, she immediately slipped outside to the shed where Buttermilk was now quartered and proceeded to pull the teats extra hard, trying diligently to please her mother by wringing out every drop.

A couple of weeks later, they were seated at supper when Roy began to complain. "Don't let Flora milk Buttermilk again! She milks the cow dry ever' cotton pickin' time! Then Buttermilk's too sore to let anybody milk her for a while."

"Yeah, and then Mommy doesn't have enough cream to make butter either." Hank piped up. "I had to eat my corn raw."

"Not raw," Rosa Lee's gentle voice corrected. "Just without butter."

"That's worse than raw!"

"That's enough!" Jake's stern voice stopped the fussing. "I didn't hear anybody else volunteering to milk the cow." Silence settled over the table.

Marina focused on her food, unwilling to see the sad faces of her children. She knew the pall that had fallen over their family was her fault. As the mother, she set the emotional tone of the house, and if she was cranky, it wasn't long until everybody else was too. She'd been testy for months now, and the kids had caught her mood. Even Jake was quieter. She knew he sensed her feeling of drowning but didn't know how to help.

The family finished eating. Rosa Lee and Emily began to clear the table. Flora hesitated and then asked, "Would you like me to milk Buttermilk, Mommy?"

"I'll do it," she answered. Her voice sounded harsher than she intended. "You go ahead and read your book," she added hoping the suggestion would soften what clearly sounded like a rebuke.

Marina stepped outside. The days were staying light longer now. "If only that could be said for my heart," she thought ruefully. She picked up the bucket, pulling the stool over to sit on it. "Okay, Buttermilk. Let's see how much milk you can give the family tonight," she murmured, patting the cow gently. It wasn't much. Buttermilk was done in five minutes, and no amount of coaxing could get another drop out of her. Marina patted her again. "You did your best, girl. Sometimes we don't have any more in us to give."

Sighing, she returned the stool to its place. She wished she could stay outside a little longer. The cool air felt calming to her soul. Too bad she no longer had plants to water around the house. There was something soothing about growing a plant for no other reason than it was beautiful. She regretted being so stubborn about the flowers and plants. She wished Jake had insisted she move them.

The night sky darkened. Still, she lingered outside. She knew what was happening in the house. Hank would be anxious because she was out so long. Sadie and Samuel might be fussing a little. Rosa Lee would comfort them. Emily would ask if she could go outside to check on Mommy, but Jake would say no. He would understand.

Marina looked up at the stars. "Please, God, please!" she murmured. "Help me find my way out of this."

Although she didn't feel anything different right then, a moment of gratitude for an understanding husband and her

173

heart crying out for help from a God who was listening, chinked the anger that was binding her.

Over the next several weeks, tiny slivers of thankfulness coaxed her to freedom. She noticed Rosa Lee, Flora, and Walt all added significantly to the cotton total at the end of the day. She paid attention that Roy, too, was a steady worker with a strong work ethic beyond his years. He didn't say much, but he kept picking. She found herself in awe of how Emily could entertain herself while picking cotton under scorching heat. That little girl imagined something pleasant in every chore. What good children they all were! Eventually, gratitude gave way to moments of joy. Without even realizing, Marina began to heal.

She went out to the far field early one October evening, looking for Sammy's shoe. It had been lost while they were picking cotton, but no one had noticed until after supper. Wanting a few minutes to herself, she directed the girls to clean the table while she went back to search.

The sun settled comfortably down on the rim of the world. Streaks of pink, purple, orange, and red stretched across the sky as though God was in a bragging mood. The fading light cast a glow over unpicked cotton fields. It was breath-taking and Marina found herself soaking in the beauty. Her heart swelled and for the first time after a long series of agonies, she felt a crystal moment. Joy had sneaked up on her when she wasn't looking.

She found the shoe where the little ones had been playing. It was perched on a cotton stalk as if it had grown there. Laughing softly, Marina stuck the shoe in her apron pocket and started back to the house.

Walking along the edge of the fields, warmed by the disappearing sun, she felt something rigid inside her dissolve. She had had enough. She was sick of the bitterness, sick of herself wallowing in it. "The thieves have taken enough. I have let them separate me from my husband and children. No one will rob me of joy anymore."

She neared the house. Her family sat on the porch, watching as she strode toward them. They looked leery. Lately they hadn't known what to expect from her.

She stopped three feet short of the porch, her eyes traveling over each beautiful face. "Get out the shovels, children. We're going to plant flowers."

Chapter Nineteen

March 1931

"You get enough pie, Pappy?" Rosa Lee asked.

"Yes'm. Two big pieces. Thank you."

"I made it special 'cause I know how much you like apple pie."

"Thank you again."

"Are you satisfied, Pappy?" Flora asked.

"More than satisfied," Jake assured them.

"That's good. We want you to be satisfied."

Marina cocked a suspicious eye at her two oldest girls. Whatever they were up to, they clearly believed they had the better shot at convincing their father.

"Those automobile cars sure are somethin', aren't they, Pappy?" Flora continued.

"Yep, they are."

"Nothing in the world like them," Rosa Lee added.

"Don't guess there is."

"All that modern science—you could even say it's educational," Flora tried to prompt her father. "You and Mommy have always been in favor of education."

"Yep," Jake agreed. "We're in favor of you knowin' how to read and write and do your figurin'." Marina saw the tinge of a smile around Jake's mouth and knew he was enjoying making them work for whatever they were after.

Rosa Lee threw a desperate look at her sister, and Flora decided to take the bull by the horns. She sat up straighter and leaned forward. "Pappy, we appreciate you makin' sure all us kids are getting' more education than you did." She paused. Jake nodded, so she continued. "Sometimes, children get opportunities their parents didn't, and that's good isn't it, Pappy?"

"Oh, not always," Jake cautioned.

Flora paused a moment, then plunged ahead. "Well, like you said, education is good." Another pause. "Automobiles are new and modern, so ridin' in one of them could be a kind of education. You ever ridden in an automobile, Pappy?"

"Nope, can't say I ever have." They had his curiosity up now, but Jake grew children the way he grew cotton—with the patience of a man who understands the world flourishes in season.

Sensing his interest, Flora rushed ahead. "We have a chance to further our education, Pappy. This Friday we can ride in an honest-to-goodness automobile."

Jake studied his daughters' faces for a moment, then dead-panned, "The school's gettin' a car to ride ya'll around in, is it?"

Flustered, both girls stammered, "No," and the truth tumbled out. "J.R. Cowlin bought a car. He and his cousin Mac would like to take us to the basketball game in it Friday night."

"Take you. . .in a *car!*" Marina exclaimed.

"Yes, ma'am." The girls turned pleading eyes to their father. "Just imagine ridin' in a car, Pappy. Wouldn't that be somethin'?"

"A car?" Marina repeated. She turned to Jake, expecting support. Instead she saw the fascination that has come over men's faces since the wheel was first invented. Sighing deeply, she flung herself out of the rocker. Once in the kitchen, she banged a few dishes around under the guise of setting the table for the next morning's breakfast.

Although she wouldn't have admitted it to Jake or the girls, by the time Friday afternoon arrived, Marina felt the excitement of a new adventure herself. The girls finished their chores early, ironed, and re-ironed their dresses until Marina shooed them out of the house. "Go brush your teeth, girls."

Rosa Lee and Flora wandered outside, snapping birch twigs off the tree. They frayed the ends and began brushing their teeth. Five minutes later, Marina looked up from where she was trimming Emily's hair on the front porch. Those girls were still brushing their teeth. She shook her head before calling Hank up to get his haircut. Then Sadie and Samuel also had their haircuts before the older girls finally moved on from brushing their teeth.

The girls stayed in the bedroom with the curtain pulled closed. "Why on earth are they takin' so long to throw a dress over their heads?" Marina fussed. The sound of hushed giggles escaped from the curtain drawn over the doorway.

"They're excited about goin' on their date tonight. I 'spect you used to spend a little time gettin' ready when I came courtin'."

"I don't recall," Marina fibbed.

"Bet your mama would recall. I'm gonna ask her next time she's here."

Marina gave him a look and changed the subject. "You sure it's safe for our girls to be ridin' in one of those automobiles?"

Jake grinned. "Wouldn't mind takin' a ride in one of 'em myself," he admitted.

Marina sighed and called out, "You girls hurry up so's those boys won't have to wait on you."

"Boys are supposed to wait on girls," Flora trilled. "It's soooo romantic." The girls' voices were lost in a new round of giggles, with Rosa Lee clearly trying to hush Flora, but getting so tickled herself she gave up trying.

The boys' arrival was announced by Hank's cheers as a 1928 Model A coupe with a rumble seat crunched over the packed dirt road.

Little brothers and sisters appeared from behind the barn, the garden, and every corner of the house. They had the car surrounded before it was parked. Marina picked up baby Lilli and followed them outside.

Sheer envy shone in the older boys' eyes. They ran their palms over the fenders as though they were checking a horse's flanks. "Look at that shine," Roy breathed. Walt whistled.

"Can I drive her?" Hank asked, confident he was capable.

Marina shushed him and reached out to pull Sammy back from the car.

"I get me one," bold little Sadie announced with determination.

Flora's date laughed, and picking Sadie up, he plopped her into the driver's seat, where she sat yanking levers and messing with the steering wheel until her pappy pulled her out.

Still, Rosa Lee and Flora had not budged from the house. Eventually, even the comments about the car wore themselves out. The Hartmanns fell silent for a moment, each looking at the car, wondering what else they could say and finding they'd already said it all.

"Sure is a nice car," Roy repeated.

"Sure is," the boys all repeated and then became silent again.

"Why don't you boys come on inside while the girls finish gettin' ready?" Jake invited. Respectfully, the boys followed the father of their dates up on the porch and into the house. At a nod from her mother, Emily brought the boys tall glasses of sweet tea.

Marina could still hear muffled giggles coming from behind the curtain. The more she heard, the madder she became. Just as she made up her mind to call them out, the curtain opened, and Rosa Lee appeared. "Mac, J.R," she greeted the boys. Her gentle voice matched the placid expression on her face. Marina looked at her eldest child and softened. It wouldn't be long before Rosa Lee started a home of her own. "Flora will be out in a couple minutes," Rosa Lee promised. "She's almost ready."

Marina scrutinized Rosa Lee's face carefully for clues as to what was going on, but found none. Wisely, Rosa Lee avoided looking at her mother and maintained the same calm, pleasant expression she always wore.

Without warning the curtain jerked back, signaling everyone to Flora's entrance. Her dress fit beautifully although her hat was a bit crooked. What puzzled Marina was that Flora had the silliest expression on her face, and her eyes looked wider than usual.

"Let's go!" Rosa Lee jumped up from her seat. Pulling her sister by the arm, she propelled the girl out the door, leaving their dates to follow. The boys barely made it to the car in time to open the door. As quickly as they could make the escape, the two couples were rattling down the dirt road.

"What on earth is the matter with those girls?" Marina fussed as she watched after them.

Jake's eyes twinkled as his toe nudged a can of tobacco they kept for company. The lid on the Bright Tiger Chewing Tobacco hadn't been screwed back on entirely straight. "I believe this is the culprit."

"Chewin' tobacco?" Marina exclaimed.

"Yes, ma'am. Looks like our girls wanted a bright and shiny smile for their first automobile ride."

"How could a little bit of tobacco rubbed on the teeth make the girls act so silly?"

"Those girls took more than a little chew to brighten their teeth. Flora's buzzin' worse than a cicada about to go courtin'."

Jake and Marina walked outside to the porch to watch the Model A fly down the lane, spitting dust to the wind. Marina shook her head in disgust. "Do you think those girls will ever have enough sense to be responsible for their own lives?"

"Oh, I think so," Jake assured her. He watched as Flora waved her cloche out the side of the car, her laughter floating across the fields like cotton seed to the wind. "All the same," he added, "maybe it would be a good idea for them to live close by. We might want to keep an eye on the grandkids."

Chapter Twenty

July 1932

Marina carried a pan of dirty dishwater out to the porch. Tipping it slightly, she watered a rosebush. Next she pulled scissors out of her apron and deadheaded several fading blooms. Then she took a moment to wrap a long trailing clematis vine around the end post.

Just beyond the front porch, she could hear Sadie and Sammy jabbering as they played in the dirt. "Sammy, we need middle names" Sadie prompted.

"What for?" her twin asked.

"So's Mommy has two names to call us when she gets mad. She could say, 'Sadie Ophelia' or 'Samuel Zechariah.' The girl did a pretty fair imitation of her mother's exasperated tone. Well, she'd heard it often enough.

"Mommy don't get mad at me," Sammy countered.

Marina stifled a chuckle. She would have liked to have swatted his little bottom right then and there, but she wanted to hear the rest of their conversation. Besides, he had a point.

Sammy continued his reasoning. "You not having a middle name never stopped Mommy from getting mad at you."

"Well," Sadie argued, exasperated he didn't understand the logic. "If we had middle names, she could get madder at me AND get mad at you."

Sammy shook his head. "I don't want Mommy mad at me. That's why I don't do nothin' to make her mad."

Marina bent her head to hide a smile, watching as Sadie crossed her arms. The little girl fixed flashing dark eyes on this errant brother. Her pale, heart-shaped face surrounded by clouds of black hair looked beautiful, but formidable. In even, deadly tones she repeated, "I want to have a middle name, and since we're twins, you need to have one too."

Sammy studied his sister. Although he had the red hair, the whole family knew Sadie was the one with the temper. After a moment's hesitation, he decided to take his chances that Mommy wouldn't get too mad at him no matter how many names he had. "We can have middle names if you want 'em, Sadie."

.   .   .

Later that evening, Marina rose from the dinner table only to be accosted by her two eldest daughters. "Why don't you and Pappy go sit on the porch?" Rosa Lee and Flora ushered their parents outside. "We're going to bring you each a big slice of chocolate cake."

"You work entirely too hard," Rosa Lee added. "Flora and I will do the dishes."

Marina sat down in her rocker and looked over at Jake. "What on earth are those girls up to now?"

Jake chuckled to himself and leaned back to watch the show.

"You're not wantin' to go up in one of those aeroplanes, are you?" Marina called after them.

"What's that, Mommy?" the girls answered as they returned and served the promised dessert.

"Your mother wants to know if you're trying to sweeten us up so you can ride in an aeroplane," Jake answered.

"An aeroplane?" Rosa Lee asked puzzled. "Why would you think that?"

"Never mind," Marina waved the distraction aside. "Where is it you want to go?"

Rosa Lee and Flora looked at each other and then back at their parents. Taking a deep breath, they answered. "To church."

"To church?" their parents echoed in unison.

"We've never stopped you girls from goin' to church," Jake said.

"We want to go to a new church," Rosa Lee explained.

"It's educational," Flora added.

185

Marina raised her eyebrows. "Where is the church you want to visit?"

"Well, it's not exactly at the church."

"What are you girls talkin' about? Spit it out!" their mother commanded.

"The Pentecostals are buildin' a grape arbor across from the school house. They're havin' a revival all next week," Rosa Lee explained.

"And who would you be goin' with?" Jake asked.

"Who?" Flora asked.

"Yes, *who*, you little owl," their mother answered. "Surely, you wouldn't think of asking us if you could go by yourselves, so *who* would be escorting you to church?"

"Mac and J.R."

"Would you be goin' in that automobile again?" Marina asked.

"No, ma'am. It's not workin' right now," Flora explained.

"The grape arbor is across from Blackwater School, only a mile's walk from here," Rosa Lee added.

Marina and Jake exchanged glances, giving almost imperceptible nods of approval. "Just don't get caught up in that dancin' and carryin' on, you hear me?" Jake instructed.

Rosa Lee leaned close to her father. Looking him straight in the eye, she lowered her voice and asked, "You know about that?"

Marina turned her head away, barely able to stop from laughing.

"Yes, I know about that," Jake assured her.

Flora pulled her older sister away into the bedroom to discuss what they would wear before she could say anything more.

Marina and Jake looked at each other, shook their heads, and began to laugh. "Hide the chewin' tobacco," Jake advised.

The boys arrived at six-thirty. This time the girls were ready to go. "Have the girls home before ten o'clock," Jake instructed them.

The heat of a long day spent choppin' cotton under the blistering sun had taken its toll. Barn chores were done. The younger children were settled in for the night. All the parents had left to do was wait for Rosa Lee and Flora to return from the revival. Marina joined Jake out on the porch. She set a pan of green beans in her lap and commenced snapping.

At nine-fifty Jake heaved himself up out of the rocker. "Let's go for a walk, Marina."

"Right now?" she asked, surprised. "The girls should be back any time."

Jake nodded. "It's possible we might run into them down the lane somewhere. Emily," he called, "your mother and I are goin' for a walk. Keep an eye on your brothers and sisters, please."

"Yes, Pappy."

It was a beautiful night. Marina stared up at the Arkansas sky wondering if she could replicate the stars' design in a quilt.

Jake took her hand as they strolled. "Do you remember our first date?"

"We walked to the carnival."

"That was a lot of years ago," he commented.

"That was a lot of babies ago," Marina corrected.

"It was mid-morning," Jake continued. "Your mama never would have let me take you out at night."

"No, sir, she wouldn't." Marina peered down the darkened road. "I would have thought we would have run into the girls comin' home by now."

Jake nodded. "I 'spect they might have lost track of time at the revival. Those Pentecostals can be pretty excitin'."

Marina frowned into the darkness. "Well, then, they'll be surprised to see us."

The faint lilt of music coaxed them toward the grape arbor. They could distinguish individual hymns, and the words were getting clearer with each step.

Soon the revival came into view. Grape vines, closely twisted together, were woven back and forth across a ceiling of two-by-fours. Almost a hundred people were crowded into pews made from split hickory logs. The preacher and song leader stood at the front.

Jake slipped off his hat and stepped under the leafy shelter. He spied his girls and their dates sitting toward the back of the congregation. He nodded, ushering Marina into a row right in front of them. Shock registered on all four faces as they realized they had missed curfew.

Turning slightly in their direction, Jake frowned. The boys were wearing hats inside a house of worship. That was downright disrespectful. With a swift movement of his index finger he motioned for the boys to remove them. The response was immediate. The fedoras were whipped off their heads and held in their hands.

The girls appeared panicked and looked to Marina for reassurance. She avoided meeting their eyes. She felt the girls needed to feel some emotional pain. Their poor father wouldn't be getting much sleep before he'd have to be back in the fields. Marina focused on the music. Those Pentecostals sure could sing.

The song finished and the congregation rose for an altar call. Jake touched her elbow and unobtrusively they slipped away from their bench. He paused before his girls' pew and with a look directed the four young people to the exit. The boys kept their hats off until they exited the grape arbor.

The walk home was not quite the romantic stroll the young people had envisioned or the parents had intentionally disrupted.

"We're sorry we're late, Pappy," Flora ventured. "We didn't realize what time it was."

Jake nodded. "I don't 'spect you did."

189

Occasionally, Marina broke the night hush by commenting on the loudness of the crickets or mentioning some task that needed doing the next day. The girls jumped on her words, trying hard to deflect the ominous feel.

Eventually, they reached home. "You girls go on in the house," Jake instructed. "I believe the boys and I'll have a word before we call it a night."

His daughters gave a nervous glance at the boys before meekly following their mother inside.

Marina could hear Jake's calm, steely voice. "Boys, I expect to be obeyed. When I tell my girls to be home before ten o'clock, they'd better be here."

"We meant to. . .," the boys protested before a look from Jake silenced the interruption.

"If you'd like to continue dating Rosa Lee and Flora, then you'd better get very good at keeping track of time. Do we understand each other?"

"Yes, sir,"

"Good-night, then." Jake opened the door, leaving two young men with the certainty they had missed a rabbit trap by a tail.

Marina smiled. No doubt about it. She had married a good man.

Chapter Twenty-One

September 1933

Rosa Lee announced she and Mac were getting married in March. Flora helped her sister hem sheets and pillowcases, cut curtains out of sugar sacks, and stuff tick full of feathers. Emily sewed kitchen towels, her stitches so small they practically disappeared into the material. Marina smiled at the sight of her girls laughing as they worked. She wondered if Flora's thoughts were also straying to marriage. She and Mac's cousin JR seemed to fight and make up so much it was hard to tell what they were going to do.

Mac and Rosa Lee moved to Lake City shortly after they married. He took a job managing a filling station. As busy as life was and with as many children as she still had running in and out of the house, Marina still missed her girl. Mac was a good man and a hard worker. She and Jake both liked him, but twenty miles was too far away! Marina worked out her loneliness by piecing the wedding ring quilt.

When Marina couldn't stand it any longer, she and Jake loaded everybody up in the wagon and headed for Lake City. Rosa Lee cooked up a big feast for the family. Afterwards, everyone meandered over to the St. Francis River to fish before loading up for the wagon ride back to Manila.

. . .

The seasons kept coming, and so did Marina's babies. A few weeks before Clara's arrival, the family was finishing up a Saturday noon meal of black-eyed peas and ham hocks. "Do you have a list of what you need at Tiger-Levine's?" Jake asked.

Marina nodded tiredly. She did not feel well this morning.

"Alright. We'll leave in fifteen minutes." He looked around the table at his children. "Ya'll be ready. I've got a lot to do in town and I don't want to have to call you twice." The children scattered to wash up.

Marina stayed seated but began stacking dishes from the table. What she wanted more than anything was to lie down on the bed. Goodness! If she took a nap in the middle of the day, it would scare the wits out of her children! Jake would probably send for the doctor. Marina laughed to herself. A family's life might revolve around the father, but it was the mother who kept everything going. Nine babies and number ten on the way!

192

After this many children, you'd think she could have a baby without even slowing down, but each pregnancy had been as different as the child. Funny, the twins had been the easiest.

Sighing, she heaved herself out of the chair. Her pregnancy had advanced from the energetic phase of whipping the house and everybody in it into shape to the *I don't think I can fit through that door* stage. "Maybe I should tell Jake he's going to need a lever and a lift to mount me on top of that wagon," she muttered.

On their way to town she felt as though the wagon would shake her to pieces, but Marina knew they were hitting the same number of potholes as at any other time. In an attempt to quiet her queasy stomach, she held her abdomen as they pulled in front of Tiger-Levine's store.

"Would you like a Dr. Pepper?" Jake asked in an obvious attempt to lift her spirits.

Surprised, Marina almost said no. They didn't need to spend money on luxuries. But the thought of a cold Dr. Pepper sounded so good. Maybe it would settle her stomach. "That'd be fine," she smiled.

"Can I go in the store with you?" Sadie begged from the back of the wagon.

"No. You kids stay here and keep your mother company." He looked at Marina, concerned. "I'll be right back."

True to his word, he returned with two opened bottles of Dr. Pepper, ice chips from the barrel still running down the glass sides. Jake handed one of the sodas over before stepping back up on the wagon.

Marina took a sip. That tasted good. She took a longer drink and could feel it settling her stomach. Jake watched in amazement as she tilted the bottle back for a third time and downed the entire drink like a boozer in town on Saturday night. Without a word, he handed over his Dr. Pepper. She accepted the bottle with undisguised eagerness. It didn't take her long to finish it off.

"My, that felt good." Marina smiled, handing the empty bottle back to Jake. "I wish I'd a known Dr. Pepper was good for morning sickness nine babies ago."

In the back of the wagon, Sadie leaned over to Sammy. "When I grow up, I'm gonna have me a baby so's I can drink me two Dr. Peppers."

. . .

Marina gave birth to Clara. A month later, Rosa Lee gave birth to Marina's first granddaughter, Maribel.

Her garden grew like her babies — fast. Summer was almost over. Mr. Tolleson stopped by to mention he'd be happy to give Walt a job any time they could spare the boy. Proud, Marina smiled. She and Jake were pleased with Walt. Last summer he challenged himself and picked three hundred pounds of cotton in one day. At only fifteen, he knew most of what it took to run a farm. Occasionally, he'd get a little full of himself, but other than aggravatin' his brothers and sisters, he did fine.

Marina slid biscuits off her baking sheet into a bread basket. She placed a freshly churned pound of butter on the table before sitting down in the chair closest to the kitchen stove. Marina glanced around. Everyone was present except Walt. That was unusual. The boy was always so hungry he was usually one of the first in his seat. She opened her mouth to call him when Walt appeared from the back bedroom and slipped into his place at the table — bare chested.

Flora gasped. Roy's surprise quickly turned to admiration. The younger brothers and sisters sat wide eyed and silent, apparently fascinated by his audacity. Embarrassed, Marina looked at her plate. Knowing that only moments before, she had mentally complimented her eldest son made her all the madder. She wanted to shake him. Jake focused on cutting his beef.

Misreading his family's reaction, Walt reveled in the silent commotion he was causing. He nodded at Roy the way he'd seen John Wayne do in the movies. He posed, forearms on the table, a lock of hair tumbling down into his eyes.

Marina shook her head. What was the boy thinking? Well, this was one misdeed his father could handle. And judging from the grim expression on Jake's face, he definitely would. A long minute passed with no one speaking.

"Marina," Jake began in a casual voice. "Are you busy this afternoon or could you go to town?"

Baffled, Marina answered, "Well, I'd planned to preserve some relish, but I could go into town if there's something you need."

"I need you to buy a shirt or two. Evidently, Walt doesn't have one, and the poor boy doesn't have a thing to cover his bare chest."

A chair scraped on the floor, and Walt excused himself. He was back in less than thirty seconds, shirt neatly tucked into his belted jeans. Not another word was said about Marina going to town.

One morning Jake took all the children but baby Clara with him to the field. As soon as Marina finished preparations for the noon meal, she planned to pack up her little sleeper and head for the fields to join them. She could get in a good three hours of choppin' cotton before she had to come back to the house to fix supper.

The cabin felt quiet, not just noiseless, but with the kind of serenity that seeps into your bones and calms your spirit. She needed these rare periods of silence regardless of how unnatural they felt. Her children were well-behaved, but sometimes she wished she could pack her pickles in a jar as tightly as eleven people living in a four-room house.

Beans and a ham bone were simmering on the stove. She'd wake Clara as soon as she tossed out this pan of dirty water. Marina hefted the dishpan, careful not to let dirty water slop over the sides. With no child available to open the screen door, she backed her way out and down the steps.

"BOO!" a voice yelled at her. Reacting without thought, Marina swung around and drenched her assailant with greasy dishwater.

"What'd you do that for?" a voice wailed.

Her heart pounding, Marina stared at ten-year-old Hank. Water rolled down his head, soaking his clothes. A stray curl of tomato peel hung over his ear.

In spite of his wails or maybe because of it, Marina began to laugh. "Why'd you sneak up behind me and shout?"

"I wanted to scare you."

"Well, you did. What are you doin' back here? Why aren't you out in the fields choppin'?"

"Pappy sent me to tell you we're makin' good progress if you want to work at the house this morning.'"

"Alright. You get in there and change your clothes. And when you're done, you get right back out there in the field and chop twice as hard. You 'bout scared the daylights out of me."

. . .

Flora and JR quarreled again. Without Mac and Rosa Lee to help patch it up, the courtship was over. A handsome, witty young man named Hugh Stewart had moved down from the hills a few years before. He swept Flora off her feet, marrying her within a year.

They would be moving again. Jake was close to felling the last acre. Clay had already picked out the next forty acres of virgin timber he wanted them to clear. Marina waited until the children were all in bed to broach the subject. She settled into the rocker beside her husband. "Jake, when my brother was over today, he mentioned Mr. Cassidy has some land for sale. Forty acres. It's already cleared. His son farmed it for about seven years, but he's moving to Little Rock where his wife's people live. The land's not up against the river like. . .like our property was," Marina swallowed hard, "but Noel says its good land. Maybe you should take a look at it."

Jake turned to look his wife square in the eye. He had buried his own sorrow at losing the farm in a determination to never allow anyone to swindle him again. "Marina, they cheated us before. They'll not do it again. I'm goin' to check on the animals." With that pronouncement, he strode off the porch to check on animals that had been put to bed hours before.

So the sharecropper lifestyle continued. Jake cleared a new lot. The boys helped him build a cabin. They planted what was cleared and cleared some more.

. . .

"Jake, I think we'd better get a couple of Dr. Peppers while we're in town."

"Why? You cookin' a ham for Sunday?"

"No," Marina broke the news gently. "I want to drink 'em."

Startled, Jake turned to face her. "Again?"

Marina sighed. "Again."

"Yes, ma'am!" Jake yelled and flipped the reins to get the mule moving.

Chapter Twenty-Two

August 1935

Marina felt guilty. Although Rosa Lee had not had any problem with her first pregnancy, she had miscarried every baby since then. Three losses — three babies. Now Marina was pregnant again. It seemed like such an affront to her dear daughter, who was born to be a mother.

In August, Flora had a baby girl she named Virginia. Two months later, Marina gave birth to a boy they called Joseph. Rosa Lee's generous spirit hid her pain, but her mother's and sister's hearts ached for her.

At the drug store one Saturday, Marina overheard two women whispering that once a woman's babies started having babies, she should stop having them. Marina's face burned. She thought she should have stopped getting pregnant too. Then she looked at her children and love overrode embarrassment. She couldn't imagine life without any one of them.

1937 came in with a flood. "We've done this before," Jake commented. "We'll make it through again." He was right. While the Army Corp of Engineers was busy tearing down levies to save the town of Cairo, Illinois, he and his older boys waterproofed the buildings and moved animals to higher ground.

Water rose to inches below the raised cabin. If they needed to leave the house, they went by boat. Or, in the case of Hank and the twins, went by bathtub. Marina looked out the window to see three of her children floating by in an old tin washtub they had dragged out of the barn. With Sadie in front, they used thick sticks to maneuver their boat through floodwaters.

After the flood, a well-meaning neighbor commented, "Well, at least you didn't lose your farm in a flood. That house Jake built back by the river is still standin'. The family livin' there now just brags about how strong it is."

Later, Marina commented to Jake. "I think I could have stood it easier if the flood had taken our home instead of losin' the farm to sheer meanness and greed."

. . .

Joey seemed to grow even faster than the other children. Soon he was eighteen months. One morning, Marina watched him determinedly trot from the hickory table to the middle of the floor. He plopped his little bottom down on the floor and peered through a crack in the floorboards. He stared intently as if he could see something others could not. Every once in a while, he would clap as if pleased with whatever show he was watching. After the third time he picked the same spot on the floor, Marina wrung out her dishrag, hung it across the dishpan, and walked over to investigate. A skinny little garden snake could barely be seen through the crack in the wooden planks. Occasionally, it would rise straight up as though greeting Joey. Delighted, he applauded. "Looks like you've made a friend," she laughed, returning to the sink and taking up her dishrag once more.

Mothering Joey was different. It wasn't that she loved him more than any of the others. She would have given her all for any one of them. In fact, she did—every day. It was just that having teenagers lightened her work load a little. She had the gift of more time to enjoy the baby of the family.

A strong boom sounded in the distance. His playmate forgotten, Joey raced to Marina, burying his head in her skirt and holding onto her legs with all his might. She disentangled him, lifting him up so they were eye to eye. "It's alright," she soothed. "Mommy won't let anything hurt you. I promise. That noise is just thunder. It's the storm's way of braggin'."

It was a boisterous autumn. Every time lightning and thunder crashed, Joey ran to find Mommy. Marina always stopped what she was doing to comfort him. It happened so often that whenever raindrops fell, she looked to see where Joey was playing. It wasn't long before he came running to her.

A couple of weeks before Joey's second birthday, Jake suggested, "Let's get Joey a wagon for his birthday."

Looking up from her darning in surprise, Marina asked. "A birthday present? We've never bought the children birthday presents before."

"We never could afford it. This was a good cotton year. I saw a red wagon over at Tiger-Levine's. Sadie and Samuel could pull the littler ones out to the cotton fields in it. That would be easier on you. All of them would have fun taking turns ridin' in it," Jake urged.

A smile crossed Marina's face as she imagined them laughing, shouting, and carrying on as they marched up and down the trail to the fields. "They'd have to keep it clean," she cautioned.

"I 'spect they'd be so tickled to have a wagon they'll be fightin' over who gets the privilege of cleanin' it," Jake predicted.

The children were disappointed not to be allowed to accompany their parents into town the following Saturday. Jake told them he and Mommy had important business to attend to. They returned about half an hour before twilight and drove the wagon straight into the barn. The children knew better than to ask questions, but whatever the important business had been, it must have turned out well. Pappy came in whistling.

Marina was peeling zucchini, smiling to herself as she anticipated the great surprise still five days off. Joey wandered into the room and tugged on her skirt. He raised chubby arms, fretting to be picked up. "What's the matter, honey?" Marina comforted him. "The sky's clear. I don't think it'll rain any time soon." She picked him up. "You feel a little warm." Joey tried to talk, but only hoarse croaks came out. "Emily, would you finish supper. I'm going to rock him. Sadie, take this rag and run out to the pump. I need a cold cloth for Joey." Marina sat down in the rocker, cuddling him close.

Dinner time came. Emily fixed a delicious meal, but Joey refused to eat. "He has a sore throat," Marina explained to Jake. "Look how swollen his glands are."

They woke several times in the night to check on him. He continued to get weaker, but his fever stayed low, never rising enough to warrant calling the doctor.

Baby Joey was everyone's pet. His brothers and sisters worried in silence.

"See how white he looks," Sadie commented.

"His skin is cold, but he's sweatin'," Emily murmured.

"Maybe he's sweatin' out the fever," Jake replied.

Marina placed her hand across Joey's chest. "Feel his heart." She looked up at her husband. Worry was written across both of their faces. "It's beatin' so fast. His little body is shakin'."

"I don't care what his temperature is. If he's not better tomorrow, we're goin' to get the doctor," Jake responded in a voice fierce with fear.

A gray, rainy November dawn brought no relief. Joey's labored breathing could be heard throughout the small cabin.

Wanting to see what was causing such thickness in his voice, Marina called for Hank to bring her a gaslight. It hurt so much for Joey to open his mouth it was difficult to get him to cooperate. Finally, they tilted him back enough to see a thick grayness covering his throat and tonsils.

"Walt!" Jake called sharply. "Get the doctor!"

"Yes, sir!" That was the command Walt had been waiting to hear. He shot out of the somber house.

In an attempt to make swallowing easier, Marina changed him from lying down in her arms to a vertical position. Thinking movement might help, she stood up, intending to walk the floor with him.

"I'll take him," Jake offered. Reluctantly, but understanding Jake also had a need to do something, Marina allowed her husband to take their son.

"I'll start breakfast." Any work was better than idleness.

Jake walked back and forth over the planks. The baby's rapid breathing slowed. Finally, Joey took a deep, wheezy breath, slowly letting it out.

"He sounds better," Emily murmured hopefully. "I don't hear those harsh sounds."

The door opened and Mr. Hall from across the road stepped inside the cabin. Water dripped off his six-foot, broad-shouldered frame. He had heard Walt tear out of the yard on the mule. Knowing the baby was ill, he came to see if he could help.

He removed his hat and stood there for a moment to study what was happening. Eyes full of sorrow, he watched as Jake, holding his son, marched back and forth, back and forth across the room. Eyes open, but no longer seeing, the little boy's head and body lay limply against the father's shoulder. Breathing had stopped.

Reluctantly, the older man crossed the room to Jake. With a heart full of compassion, Mr. Hall gently reached up, taking Joey out of Jake's arms. "He's gone, Jake. He's gone." Almost ceremoniously, Mr. Hall laid the baby down on the sofa before covering the entire head and body with a soft blanket.

Jake stared at his empty arms, arms that had held his son so tight. Why hadn't that been enough? Why couldn't he have held on to him tighter? How could he have allowed *anything* to pull his son away from him? Jake's strength crumbled. He turned, pushing open the door. In long, angry strides he stalked across the yard to the barn, smacking open the stable door, leaving it to slam behind him. For a moment, they heard nothing. Then, from the barn came a wail of grief too severe for the father to utter in words.

Unable to feel anything, Marina froze. Her heart had not yet comprehended Joey's death. She thought only about needing to comfort Jake. She started toward the door when Mr. Hall caught her by the arm and shook his head. "Leave him be, Marina," he cautioned. "There's times when a man needs the freedom to pour out his sorrow in the wilderness."

The unnaturalness of outliving her child muddled Marina's thinking. Lost, she looked around the room. The sofa was empty; Joey was gone. Flora had taken the little body to the back room to clean and prepare him. Marina could hear the scrape of drawers being opened and shut as Flora pulled out clothes to dress her baby brother for burial. Grief rushed in upon her.

The wind cut hard the day of the funeral. It whipped across the faces of the Hartmann family, etching in loss that would last a lifetime. The Manila cemetery had grown since they had last been there, spreading out across the east side of town. Marina stood under a tall oak, registering nothing but the incomprehensible pain of a mother burying her child.

After the funeral, Jake focused on work, fiercely intent on wiping out his searing anguish. Marina was silent, withdrawn, clutching a sorrow that could not be thrown away. No one talked about it, but grief chiseled its imprint on every member of the family.

The day of the first storm since Joey's death caught Marina off guard. She was stretched over a fat feather bed, tucking a fresh fitted sheet under the mattress corner when dry lightning flashed outside the window. Automatically, she looked up to see where Joey was so he wouldn't be afraid. Then she remembered and the desolation hit her as if for the first time.

Finishing the bed, she walked outside on the porch, her eyes straining to the northeast and the cemetery where Joey lay buried under a big oak tree. Black menacing clouds forming a murky line revealed a storm brewing east of town. The farm felt clammed up with an unnatural silence that mocked calm.

"Mommy!" a voice called. Turning, she saw Roy running in from the fields. "Pappy says we're to get the animals in the barn and rope the doors to hold 'em. He says this storm's gonna be a nasty one."

"I'll send Hank out to help you," she promised. Opening the screen door, she called instructions to the children. They obeyed immediately, leading the cows in from the woods, moving the porch rockers and potted plants inside, catching the chickens, and transferring them to the safety of the barn. Jake and the boys made it back to the house. Marina couldn't help herself. Once everyone and everything was safe inside, she slipped out the screen door again, watching from the front porch as the storm gathered for its primal blitz.

Angry clouds twisted in the sky before throwing down their first barrage of watery artillery. The wind screamed its battle cry, battering the barn, howling in frustration. Cold rain blew across the fields, freezing drops into slashing bits of ice. Marina watched, the bombardment of raging sleet mirroring her internal storm. Tears rained down in a torrent of their own as she sobbed for the child she could no longer comfort.

Months passed without their returning to the cemetery. Jake always had a reason why they shouldn't go to town that Saturday. Marina knew he was avoiding visiting the grave. Her heart suffered. She yearned to be there.

Eventually, they needed planting supplies, and a trip to town was required.

They couldn't afford a stone, but Jake had crafted a beautiful wooden marker. He carved in Joey's full name, birthdate, and date of death. With a heavy sigh, he now loaded it into the wagon.

They entered Manila Cemetery. Jake pulled Ol' Jeb up short under the tall arch marking the entrance. The storm's wrath had decimated sections of the graveyard, tossing aside tombstones, changing the landscape. The cemetery appeared scarred, as if some giant hand had snatched out patches of bushes and knocked down lines of trees. The town's people had already cleaned up after the storm. Fallen trees had been carted away. The cemetery felt still, empty.

Marina stretched her neck to pick out the oak where Joey lay. It wasn't there. Confused, she inspected tree after tree. That couldn't be right. Joey's oak was much taller. The branches of his tree spread out farther. She racked her memory for clues. Nothing looked the same.

Neither of them said anything for several moments, until in a tormented whisper, Marina asked, "Where is he?"

Not a trace of Joey's grave remained. Marina had lost him again.

Chapter Twenty-Three

August 1938

"Where's Pappy?" Roy burst into the house. His breath came in heavy gasps from having run so fast. Seventeen years old, he carried a smaller frame than his older brother Walt but could match him on determination. Roy had always been their most serious child. Right now, he appeared seriously mad enough to whip somebody.

"What's the matter?" Marina asked, looking up from kneading bread.

"You know that triangle patch of corn off the east side of the forty?"

"Yes. It's so far off by itself, your father was afraid the deer might get it."

"Well, the deer didn't get it, but somebody did."

"What do you mean?" Marina spoke sharply, her hands still working as she concentrated on what Roy was saying.

"I was comin' home from fishin' and decided to check to see if the corn is ripe. The ditch kind of separates it off by itself, so I'm not out there as often. The outside rows looked good, so I walked in farther to check the center rows. The stalks are standing there, but the ears of corn are gone. Whoever stole the corn left the outside edges of the field alone, so it'd look like nobody's been there. There's not a leaf bent on the three outside rows. On the inside of the patch that lousy crook stole every ear of corn he could get his hands on!"

"Your father's out by the barn. You'd better go tell him." Roy gave a quick nod and raced down the worn path. Marina plopped the ready dough into the bread pan, washing up the bowl and clearing the counter before she followed them to the triangle patch.

Jake didn't say much as he toured row after row of stripped stalks. A grim expression steeled his face as he contemplated who would have stolen from him. It didn't appear to be the "borrowing" of hobos, who generally took one ear from several stalks. They tried to avoid notice.

This was clearly the work of someone who wanted a cushion of time between the theft and the discovery so there would be a greater number of people to suspect. That meant the thief was one of a small group of suspects. Sharing the corn didn't bother him. Jake was a generous man and this patch barely amounted to a crooked half acre. What Jake couldn't abide was sneakiness.

211

Roy followed his father up one row and down the next, pointing out every broken stalk and missing ear. After Jake inspected the damage, he stood for a moment looking at the ground, then announced, "Alright. Let's get back to work."

"Back to work!" Roy protested. "Pappy, they stole our corn! What are we goin' to do about this? Somebody needs to pay!"

"They won't be payin' today," Jake answered, walking back towards the barn.

Roy ran to catch up with him. "That was our corn! Walt and I planted it. Nobody had a right to take it. I want to make 'em pay." Roy had a strong sense of justice. Marina also suspected he was livid that the thief thought he had outwitted them.

"Roy," Jake's quiet voice took on a stern tone that put an end to any thoughts of further discussion. "There's not a thing more we can do about this right now. Whoever took that corn is either long gone or will do something else to let us know he's here. Be patient, son. Keep your eyes open."

"Yes, sir." Roy heard his father's words *"be patient and keep your eyes open"* as if they were battle strategy. Roy knew how to be patient. That discipline was what made him good at checkers. He took the time to think out every possible move available to his opponent. He also knew how to keep his eyes open. There wasn't much that happened on the farm without Roy knowing about it. Noting the determined set of her son's mouth, Marina suspected the thief had met his match.

The thief struck again the first night of corn harvest. This time corn was missing from the barn. The thief had pried open a barn window and taken every ear he could touch without actually coming into the barn. Roy's eyes blazed with anger. He suggested he be allowed to sit up all night waiting for the thief with a gun.

Jake listened to the report. "I don't think a gun will be necessary. Catch him in the act."

Roy disappeared into the barn where he stayed until suppertime. When he finally emerged, his eyes glinted with satisfaction.

Nothing happened for several days. Then one morning before breakfast Roy came running in from barn chores. "I got him. Caught him red-handed!"

"Where is he now?" Jake asked.

"The barn. He's not going anywhere."

With Roy in the lead, the Hartmann clan headed for the barn. Stepping into the dark, it took a moment for their eyes to adjust. A whimpering sound came from the far end of the building. Mule Sullivan stood on the outside of the barn wall, his right arm caught in a trap set to trip the moment he put his arm through the window to grab some corn. He saw Jake and began to talk fast. "Jake, you gotta help me. My arm's caught. I need you to get me out of this mess. Your boy here won't unlock this trap. I need my arm back. I been like this since midnight."

"Mule," Jake greeted him easily. "I'm surprised to see you. Usually you knock at the front door when you stop by. What're you doing in here?"

"I needed to borrow some corn. . .didn't want to bother you at breakfast."

"Been standing there since midnight, did you say?"

"Yeah. I just needed some corn. Times have been hard, Jake. I didn't think you'd miss a couple of ears."

"Don't 'spect I would've missed a couple of ears. 'Course, that patch on the backside of the forty is a little more than a couple of ears."

Mule's eyes widened in fear from having been discovered. "Don't know what yer talkin' 'bout on the backside. . . ." He saw the look in Jake's eyes and his voice trailed off. Swallowing hard, he started again. "I got to feed my family," he whined. "You feed your family!" He said it almost like an accusation.

Jake nodded. "We work hard to put food on the table." It was a quiet indictment of Mule's known laziness. "Mule, I'm your neighbor. If you need corn, you come to me like a man, and I'll help you." He paused and in calm, unmistakably resolute tones warned, "Don't you ever steal from my family again." He looked deep into Mule's eyes. "Do we understand one another?"

"Yes, sir. I know just what you mean."

Jake unhooked a burlap sack from the wall. With swift motions he filled it full of his best eating corn. Handing it to

Mule, he said, "Now this is for your family. Make sure they get it." He nodded to Roy. "Let him loose."

The moment his arm was free, Mule grabbed the sack of corn and fled.

.   .   .

Talk of America joining the European war filled town and family discussions. A thread of fear wound its way into Marina's heart. What if her boys were drafted? What if one of them signed up? She silently turned these ideas over and over in her heart as she went about her tasks.

Marina was bent over her sewing when a scream from the yard pierced the air. Every child's cry is different, and Marina recognized six-year-old Clara's. Family members jolted into action. She ran from the house as Jake bolted from the barn. Lilli was standing under the big tree out front. Clara lay in a crumpled heap in the dirt.

Marina dropped to the ground beside her youngest daughter. "Are you alright?"

"No," Clara sobbed.

Marina heaved a sigh of relief. Clara could talk. "Tell me where it hurts. Did you hit your head?"

"No," the sobbing continued.

Jake felt Clara's arms and legs checking for breaks. "Tell me where you hurt," he demanded.

215

"My. . .my. . .my. . .bot. . .tom!"

Marina and Jake looked at each other, relief almost giving way to laughter.

Jake noticed an upturned bucket and a two-by-six lying in the grass. "What were you doing?"

"We. . .we. . .were. . .jumpin' boards. . .and Lilli. . .she jumped. . .too hard." With the last word a fresh avalanche of tears poured out.

"Oh, she's not hurt so bad," Lilli grumbled, hoping to minimize her own complicity. A swift look from her father convinced her to change tactics. "All we were doin'," she explained, "was jumpin' boards." Seeing the confused look on his face, she continued. "You lay a board over an upside down bucket. I was standing on this end of the board. Clara was on the other. I jumped first. Clara went up in the air. She came down and hit the board, so I went up." Lilli wiggled her hand in seesaw fashion to illustrate. "Back and forth."

Clara inserted herself back into the conversation. "Then Lilli jumped too hard, and I fell down and hurt my bottom." Fresh tears rolled, a few of which, her mother guessed, were intended to ward off punishment.

"Hush now," Marina commanded. "You're a little sore, but you'll be alright."

Jake wasn't sure whether he was mad at Lilli for coaxing her little sister to jump boards or madder at Clara for scaring the daylights out of them. "You think you're in trouble now, you're

really going to be in a pickle if I catch either one of you jumpin'
boards again. Do you understand me?"

"Yes, sir," his girls chorused.

Marina set Clara on her feet, dusted her off, and sent the
girls to put away the board and bucket. She shook her head.
"Time's not aging me as fast as our children's mischief is."

Thursday was wash day. Marina gathered laundry supplies while Emily and Sadie bundled piles of dirty clothes in
sheets and brought them outside. "Sadie, pump some water
for the kettle. Emily, grab the rub board and start scrubbin'
those whites."

A few minutes later, Marina lit a fire under the kettle and
dropped in homemade lye soap. The water boiled, suds foaming
up around the mouth of the kettle. Using a three-foot wooden
paddle shaped like a flat spoon, she stirred the pot. Once the
whites were scrubbed, Emily poured out the water and Sadie
rinsed them in a wash tub, twice. Steam rose up, blending with
sweat before it dripped back down their faces. All morning
long, loads of clothes and sheets repeated the pattern: scrub,
boil, rinse, rinse again, hang on the line, scrub, boil, rinse, rinse
again, hang on the line. Laundry was such hard work. Thank
goodness it's only one day a week, Marina thought as she
pinned the last pair of pants to the clothesline.

She was clearing the dinner table when the suspicious sound
of a board slapping against the ground caught her attention.
Drying her hands on a dish towel, she met Jake's eyes, motioning

him to follow her to the window. Outside the window Lilli and Clara had propped the two-by-six plank on top of a bucket and were back at their old game.

"What are those children thinkin'?" Marina shook her head. "They could play house, jacks, tag, any number of games that would not get them into trouble, yet here they are jumpin' boards again."

The grim look on Jake's face informed her he was taking time to calm down before responding to his daughers' disobedience. He sympathized with a desire for independence, but flat out defiance was never ignored.

Lilli's feet hit the board, sending Clara up. When the board tilted in her direction, Clara was ready. Her shoes stomped the board with every ounce of power in that little body. The result was more powerful than mischievous Clara had hoped for. Lilli flew off the board at an angle.

Marina caught her breath, ready to run to her daughter, but Jake placed a restraining hand on her shoulder, pointing back out the window. Lilli had landed in the empty wash kettle. She was struggling to get out, but was stuck. Clara was laughing too hard to help.

Marina shook her head, giving a little chuckle. "You're not going to whip her after that, are you?"

"Well, I have to keep my promise, and I did say she was going to be in a pickle if I caught her jumping boards again." Jake studied his daughter, her bottom still stuffed in the wash kettle, bony arms and legs sticking straight up, not unlike pickles poking out of a jar. He shook his head, no longer able to hold back the laughter. "Seems I can ignore this one 'cause she kept my promise all by herself."

Chapter Twenty-Four

April 1940

Marina cut worn out towels into washrags, darning darns and patching patches as the Great Depression straggled on. Work, even sharecropping, was almost impossible to find. Flora's husband, Hugh, gave up hunting for a local job and joined the army. Flora and their two children, Virginia and Lonnie, moved in with her parents. Lilli and Clara took Virginia along to school with them on the first day. Even though Ginny was only four, she was able to read, so the teacher let her stay.

With half-a-dozen assorted-sized dresses slung over her arm and a pocketful of wooden clothespins in her apron, Marina commenced hanging the clothes up to dry. Her hand pinned the family's laundry while her head planned their supper. She had meat left over from Sunday that could be cut up for creamed chipped beef over toast. With the way those boys of hers could eat, there wasn't much meat left to "chip off." Every one of the boys had a hollow leg and a couple of the girls too. Well, she'd make do.

The sound of an automobile caused Marina to turn her head toward the road. Coming up the packed dirt road was a 1938 blue Chevrolet. She shaded her eyes until she could see Miss Perkins, the teacher up at Blackwater School, behind the wheel. Miss Perkins was a career teacher. She had taught school at Blackwater since the current students' parents were students. Marina grabbed the last of her laundry out of the basket. Tossing garments over the clothes line, she pushed down the wooden pins to secure them on the line and then headed to the porch to meet her guest.

Why on earth would Miss Perkins stop by the house? Wouldn't be for a visit. A proper lady like her would never waste time chatting over a cup of coffee without a purpose. Might be one of the children had gotten into some trouble. No one had looked particularly guilty when they got in from school today although Hank had offered to chop some firewood without being asked. Marina sighed. That boy! He'd been a trial to teachers since the first day he took his pet frog to school. You'd have thought he'd have learned his lesson when the teacher spanked him and Jake did too. Jake always told the children, "You misbehave and get a spankin' at school, I'll follow it up with another one at home." Marina hastened her pace. Whatever had happened, had happened. Best find out the worst and deal with it.

"Miss Perkins, nice of you to drop by."

"Thank you, Mrs. Hartmann." A pert hat rested on rolls of graying brown curls. The teacher held herself with perfect posture. She wore a fitted blue dress with a V-neck and large white buttons down the front. Her slightly puffed sleeves were trimmed in white and matched the collar. While most single and married women were addressed as 'Miz', everyone in the county called Amelia Perkins *Miss Perkins*. Miss Perkins insisted on it. Marina admired her greatly.

The teacher spoke in clear, precise tones. "I wonder if I could have a word with you."

"Surely. Why don't we have a seat up here?"

Miss Perkins followed Marina up to the porch and sat down in Jake's rocker. A slight tension ran through their interactions, neither woman sure of the outcome of this conversation.

The door opened and wide-faced Clara peeked out. "Clara, go get us glasses of sweet tea, please," Marina instructed. Without a word, the door banged shut and the girl disappeared inside. Teacher and mother smiled tensely at each other while they waited for the necessary hospitality to be completed.

When Clara returned, Miss Perkins took a sip of tea before setting the glass down. Clearly believing she had met her social obligations, she launched into the conversation she had prepared. "Mrs. Hartmann, I've come about Lilli."

Marina blinked and sat up straighter. Lilli! What on earth could Lilli have done to create a ruckus? At age ten, she was still so shy she barely spoke to anyone outside her own family. Marina was always having to push her forward to greet neighbors they met in town. Still, Marina knew none of her children was beyond mischief. "What has Lilli done?"

"She played the piano," Miss Perkins announced. She sneaked in at recess when all the children were supposed to be outside. I was down the hall in the office. I heard the sound of music and went to investigate. I thought perhaps it was one of the other teachers, but it was Lilli. She played for several minutes and never noticed me standing there. She was completely in her own little world. I couldn't believe it!"

"I'm sorry about that, Miss Perkins. Lilli loves music. She's always tappin' away on the table pretendin' she's a pianist."

"It wasn't just that one day, Mrs. Hartmann. I started watching her. She sneaks in from recess to play the piano every day. The only time she didn't was when it was raining so hard none of the children were allowed to go out. And frankly, Lilli looked a little put out that the other students had interfered with her practice schedule."

Embarrassed her daughter had put herself forward like that, Marina nodded. "I'll speak to her about it. She won't do it again."

"No! You don't understand," Miss Perkins protested. "I *want* her to play. She has such an obvious passion for music. Is there any way she could take lessons? She's welcome to continue practicing at the schoolhouse."

With a mixture of pride in her daughter's accomplishment and sadness at the knowledge lessons weren't possible, Marina shook her head. "No, I'm afraid not."

"I'll teach her myself," Miss Perkins begged. "She must learn to play."

"Thank you kindly, but we do not take charity."

Miss Perkins saw her error and immediately backpedaled. "Oh, I didn't mean *charity*. I was thinking. . .twenty-five cents a lesson."

Twenty-five cents a lesson! Why Polly Patrice Cox paid $1.50 per week for her two daughters' music lessons. Marina knew so because the woman had complained about it in that bragging tone she used. Hope surged forward in Marina's heart. Twenty-five cents each week. How could she come up with it? Her mind spun with possibilities, almost immediately eliminating each one. Miss Perkins sat still, not a movement, nor a word.

Finally, Marina hit upon a solution. Selling a gallon of milk to the neighbors would bring in a quarter per week. In the past, Marina had always been reluctant to sell their milk. With such a big family, they drank most of it, and what they didn't, Marina churned for butter. She considered the possibility. It wouldn't hurt those boys to drink more water. They might fuss little, but they could do it. Marina nodded, dignity showing in the firmness of her decision. "Twenty-five cents a week would be fine, Miss Perkins."

"We're agreed then. Please tell Lilli I'll see her every Tuesday directly after school. She'll need to practice at least thirty minutes a day." The teacher added, "Although I don't expect getting her to practice will be a problem."

"No, I don't expect it will." Both women smiled.

Mission accomplished, Miss Perkins stood up, leaving her glass of sweet tea untouched except for that initial, socially-required sip. She descended the porch steps before turning around to add one last comment. "Lilli really does have a gift."

She has a gift. The words echoed in Marina's mind forcing her thoughts back to the memory of a small cabin on the banks of Big Lake. She had been eight when the traveling salesman had come through, and her parents had agreed she should have a piano. They arranged to buy it on time.

She still remembered seeing it arrive on a flatbed wagon. After the instrument was brought inside the cabin, the salesman showed her how to pick out a melody on the keys. "She has a gift," he told her parents.

Her grandfather, Doc Bauer, happened to be visiting that day. He laughed. "That's salesman talk for you," he dismissed the compliment.

In the closest Hattie ever came to talking back to her father, she answered in a mild voice, "I 'spect the salesman knows a lot about this sort of thing."

Without conscious thought, Marina's fingers tapped the porch railing, her mind plunking out the first few tunes she had learned almost forty years before. How she had loved that piano! Every day she had raced through her chores to have more time on the bench. Indulgent in this one thing, Marina knew Hattie must have quietly corrected poorly done chores that she would have normally sent Marina back to redo.

Her father had also made sacrifices so she could play piano. During the week before the salesman was scheduled to stop by for payment, Papa would go out extra early and shoot ducks to sell at market. He teased Marina, claiming he hunted special "piano ducks" that flew before dawn.

And then, Marina's father died. An accident on the riverboat sending him into icy water, a deadly bout with pneumonia, and he was gone. It felt as though every good thing Marina loved was gone with him. She still remembered the shock she felt when the piano salesman came for the last time. "My husband passed this week," Hattie informed him. "We can't afford this piano any more. You'll need to take it back."

"But you're only one more payment away from owning it," the salesman protested. "I can come back next month. You can pay me then."

Hattie shook her head. With three children to feed, a fourth baby due, and no income, realism overrode any inclination towards sentiment. "We don't have the money today. We won't have it next month neither. You best take the piano with you now."

The salesman glanced at Marina and tried one last time. "But the girl, she has such a gift."

"Draggin' it out and lettin' her stew about it for a month will only make matters worse," Hattie answered with as much gentleness as her own heavy heart could muster. "Best you take it now," she repeated.

Looking as guilty as if he were stealing from a child, the salesman loaded the piano up on the wagon and took it away.

That had been a long time ago. Marina brushed away the memory with the same resolve her mother had taught her to use brushing away tears. Well, now she had a new memory to replace that painful one. Her daughter had a gift.

With Miss Perkins gone, Marina returned to her laundry. She still had two basketfuls to hang. She glanced up at the sky and frowned. A gust of wind had picked up and the clouds seemed to be gathering. Well, maybe a feisty breeze would dry everything quick before it rained. She balanced a laundry basket on her hip so she could brush her hair back off her forehead. Then she rebalanced the basket of wet towels and continued to the clothesline. Except for an old tom cat, the yard was deserted. Never mind. They'd all show up in time for supper.

She was pinning up her third towel when she heard a wolf whistle. Startled, she whirled around. The only person anywhere in sight on that dusty road was an old bachelor named Merle Bowler. He doffed his hat and gave her a big smile. Vexed, she turned back to the clothesline without acknowledging him.

She bent over and was reaching for a fourth towel when she heard the wolf whistle again. How insulting! She grabbed her basket of wet towels and headed for the house. Marina had one foot on the porch step when she heard giggling. She paused, glancing down in the direction from which the sound came. Just barely through the wooden slats, she glimpsed a flash of blue and yellow cotton underneath the porch. The wolf whistle sounded again and this time she identified the culprit. "You two girls come out from under there!" she commanded.

Well aware the fun was over, Lilli and Virginia crawled out. "What do you have to say for yourselves?" Marina asked.

"Virginia's practicin' her whistlin', Mommy," Lilli's soft voice explained. "Ginny likes to whistle."

"Virginia! Don't you know well-behaved girls never whistle?"

Flora's little girl shook her curls.

"Well, they don't. Whistlin' is bad manners. Oh, that poor Mr. Bowler. I was plain rude to him, thinkin' he was the one who whistled. All the man did was doff his hat and smile. I'd like to apologize to him, but I sure can't tell him what I was thinkin'. What a mess!"

The two girls continued staring up into Marina's face, clearly waiting to hear their punishment. "Well, the two of you go play somewhere and no whistlin'!"

"Yes, ma'am." Lilli grabbed Virginia's hand, pulling her in the direction of a fast escape.

"And stay out from under that porch too!" Marina raised her voice to call after them.

"Yes, ma'am," they chorused again just before disappearing around the corner of the house.

Marina watched them go, then muttered to herself, "Good grief! What on earth am I going to do the next time I see Mr. Bowler?" Fussing, she picked up her basket and hurried back to hanging towels. Having a visitor today had put her behind schedule, but it was worth it. Those towels would need to hang until after supper. She glanced back up at the sky again, hoping the rain would hold off. So far the weather was cooperating.

Creamed chipped beef seemed to hit the spot with everybody at supper. After cleaning the kitchen and doing the milking, Marina decided the clothes should be about dry. She headed outside.

The children had all finished their nightly chores and were enjoying the thrill of a gusty twilight. Roy, Hank, and Sammy were pretending to be cowboys, slinging their ropes to lasso cattle only they could see. Emily sat on the porch, clearly daydreaming about that boy John she'd been talking about. Sadie, Lilli, Clara, and Virginia were all dancing in the wind. Marina remembered from her own childhood how strong winds whipping across the land stirred the imagination and made one believe almost anything could happen.

She pulled off the dry towels, smiling with contentment. Lilli would have piano lessons.

Strong gusts flapped a towel out of reach. Marina glanced up. A dirty green tinted the sky. Worried, she glanced around looking for Jake and noticed Flora's three-year-old Lonnie traipsing after his Grandpa. "Emily!" she yelled. "Get the little ones inside!" Emily rose from her reverie to obey. The boys continued to whoop it up.

Marina opened her mouth to warn Jake that Lonnie was behind him. Another gust of wind tossed her words away. As she watched, Lonnie's little body rose in the air, carried by a spiraling whirlwind. She tried to move toward her grandson but felt a wall of wind push her back. She could still see him. He was a foot off the ground, then two. His feet dangled behind Jake's back as he continued to rise. Marina didn't know if it was instinct or perhaps a sound he heard, but Jake swung around. She could see the horror on his face as he realized Lonnie's feet were inches above his head. With all the strength from a lifetime of daily swinging an axe and pushing a plow, Jake reached up and grabbed hold of Lonnie's legs, pulling him down and crushing the boy against his chest.

Marina yelled for the older boys. This time her words carried and they all ran for the safety of the house. Just as the last one reached the porch, nature held a moment of silence. Then the clouds frowned in fury and drove giant sheets of rain across the farms surrounding Manila.

Chapter Twenty-Five

June 1940

E ven the blue sky looked washed out and littered with clouds. Marina felt as depressed as the economy. They were getting by — plenty of food from the garden — but no cash for anything that required purchase. None, not even for coffee. Her mind went back over last week's conversation. She had placed a steaming mug on the table in front of Jake before sitting down in her chair. He was usually in such a hurry to get out to the fields that she hadn't thought he would notice, but he did. "Where's your coffee?"

"Oh, I don't want any this mornin'," she brushed off the question. He looked at her curiously and was about to ask why when she forestalled the question by telling him her brother Frank was coming for a visit from St. Louis next week.

A few days later, she couldn't avoid the question. "Marina, would you mind fixin' me another cup of coffee?"

She hesitated. "There isn't any more coffee, Jake. We drank the last of it'."

He looked at her steadily. "Is that why you haven't been drinkin' coffee of a mornin', so's I could have it longer before we ran out?"

"Well, you need it more than I do. You get those awful headaches when you don't have coffee."

"I'll be alright."

But he hadn't been. When he thought she wasn't looking, she caught him rubbing his temples or pinching the bridge between his eyes. If only she could grow coffee as she did vegetables!

Jake had been eight days without coffee now. She racked her brain trying to think of a way to earn money for the roasted beans. She'd tried substituting chicory. It grew wild, so she roasted and ground the root. Jake drank it manfully and did his best not to make a face, but on the third day she caught him pouring it out when he thought she wasn't looking.

They were out of meat too, but that didn't matter quite so much. She grew enough beans and in another month they would slaughter a pig. They would have enough pork to last them through the winter.

Jake and Sammy were going hunting today. Sammy was as good a hunter as his father. His father claimed Sammy was even better. The forty acres they currently lived on was already cleared. In fact, so much of Mississippi County had been deforested that wildlife was becoming scarce. When hunters went far enough out, they still brought something home, but it was likely to be only a couple of fat rabbits.

But the coffee! There was nowhere to hunt it. She looked to the bedraggled heavens. "Please God! I need one dollar to buy Jake some coffee. Just one dollar." No voice answered her. The wind blew even the cloud litter away.

When Jake and Sammy returned from their hunting trip, they walked into the kitchen looking infinitely pleased with themselves. "Well, from the expressions on your faces, I'm thinkin' you bagged a deer," Marina speculated.

"No, ma'am. We shot four fat rabbits and found something even better than a deer," Sammy informed her.

"What could be better than a deer?" she asked, curious.

Jake reached into his pocket and pulled out a dollar bill. "Found this layin' on the ground. Nobody else around for almost a mile so there's no way to find whoever lost it." He grinned. "I don't know what in the world we'll do with a whole dollar."

"I do." Marina reached over and took the money. "That dollar will buy you a pound of coffee." Jake and Sammy laughed, then went on inside to clean up. Marina glance out the window at a sky that now seemed full of clouds. "Maybe somebody did hear me," she mused.

. . .

Marina enjoyed having Flora living with them at home. She loved Virginia and Lonnie too. Grandchildren were different. Flora had all the responsibility while Marina and Jake just got to love on them. At least, that's what Marina thought until the rocker was scratched. No one would admit guilt, so Jake lined Sadie, Samuel, Lilli, and Clara up in a row giving them each a spanking. The crying was awful and it all came from Virginia. Bewildered, Jake asked, "Why are you cryin'? I didn't even spank you."

"You didn't spank me 'cause you don't love me like you do them!" she sobbed, broken-hearted.

"Bend over," he demanded.

Virginia complied but looked up and instructed, "Not too hard, Grandpa."

Jake stifled a chuckle and swatted her lightly on the bottom. Virginia straightened up and went happily out to play.

. . .

The days were hard, but they were good and full of satisfaction. Marina poured another quart of water into the pot of dried pinto beans that had been soaking all night. She didn't have quite as much salt pork to add as she would have liked but threw in what there was. To make up the difference, she tossed in extra celery stalks and a couple of onions. It would do.

"Mommy!" Flora called. Marina heard the fear in her daughter's voice. Half drying her hands on her apron she moved quickly to the living room where Flora sat rocking her two -year-old. She had stripped off all his clothes except for a diaper. "He's burnin' up, Mommy! What should I do?"

Marina kissed Lonnie's forehead and felt his arms. "I can feel the fever. We need to get it down." She looked around for the first available child. "Clara, you and Lilli take that dishpan out and pump it full of water. Try not to spill any. Set it up on the table when you come back. Virginia, bring me two towels." Each child scuttled off to obey.

Marina spread one of the bath towels out across the table. Hearing Lilli and Clara struggling, she met them at the screen door, grasping the tub by its sides. Once the tub lay on the towel, Flora gently lowered the boy into the water. Lonnie immediately went from listless to screaming at the top of his lungs.

Flora started to jerk her son out of the tub, but Marina patted her hand. "It's alright. He's so hot, the water feels freezin' to him even though it's not. I know it's hard for you to do, but we have to get this fever down or it'll injure his brain."

Clearly in as much anguish as her son, Flora lowered him back into the water. His angry eyes flashed, portraying as much indignation as his lungs did. He felt betrayed.

Marina cupped a little water in her hand. Holding it over his head and shoulders, she let it trickle down. He screamed louder. They continued the bath for a good ten minutes.

Glancing over, Marina saw big sister Virginia gripping the back of a chair, her eyes wide, never leaving her little brother. It crossed Marina's mind that Virginia had the same expression on her face that she had worn when Joey got sick. Joey and Virginia had been almost the same age and were together every day. For the first time she wondered how Joey's death might have impacted Virginia. People always said children couldn't remember events from when they were so young, but Marina wondered.

"That's enough," she announced abruptly. Taking the remaining towel, she wiped him off before grabbing a light sheet to wrap him in. "Take him in there and sit by the window, Flora. You'll get a good cross breeze to keep him cool."

Lonnie's fever stayed down for about fifteen minutes before spiking back up. This time Marina was ready with a rosemary concoction she had learned from Hattie. She had boiled the wild herb, added a little sugar to entice him to drink it, and then cooled the mixture. He made a face at the unfamiliar taste and pushed it away. Flora dabbed some on his lips, desperate to get any of drink down him.

The third home remedy they tried was a warm drink. Marina mixed up yarrow, elderberry flowers, mint, and water. Lonnie cooperated with this one even less. Virginia now sat at Flora's feet, running quickly to rewet the cloths her mother placed on his forehead, legs, back of neck, and feet. Flora tried draping one over his head. He shook it off so violently that she was afraid his temper would send the fever higher.

Roy, now age nineteen, ran over to Hattie's sharecropping cabin for a jar of his grandmother's elderberry vinegar. That generally acted as a great elixir for adults but was difficult to get down children. Lonnie rejected it at the first smell.

Having done all she could think to do, Marina went on with her chores. She jumped onto the milking stool. This felt like losing Joey all over again, even down to the wagon. They had bought one for Joey, but he died three days before his birthday. This year after Jake's last load to the cotton gin, he had splurged to buy Lonnie a red Radio Flyer for Christmas. It was over there behind the hay stack. Now he might never even see it. Suddenly, it felt so important that Lonnie get his wagon now and they not wait until Christmas. "Hurry up, girl," Marina urged the cow. She was anxious to talk to Jake about giving Lonnie the wagon early.

At her mother's suggestion, Flora brought Lonnie outside. They stood on the stoop watching as the other children in the family paraded the wagon from barn to the porch. Virginia scrambled into the wagon, and Flora settled Lonnie into his sister's arms. The others took turns pulling the wagon. In spite of their good intentions, he remained listless. After a few minutes the cheering died down.

Lonnie's fever lasted through the night, breaking at the first light of dawn. It disappeared as mysteriously as it had come, leaving the family perplexed, but grateful.

. . .

On the evening of September 21, 1940, Walt and his bride stopped by the house on their way back from the courthouse in Blytheville. Walt had married a tall, willowy girl from town. "Congratulations!" Marina and Flora hugged them both. Jake slapped his son on the back and gave his new daughter-in-law a big smile. Always one to show his emotions through action, Roy led their mule out to the barn so he could groom and water the animal for them.

Marina ushered everybody to the kitchen table, explaining, "Emily and Hank took Sadie and Samuel to a basketball game up at the school house. They'll all be sorry they missed you." She lit an extra gas lamp and boiled coffee while Flora cut large slices of buttermilk pie.

Marina and Jake listened as Walt shared their plans to share-crop less than a mile away. Shy, Nora looked down most of the time, occasionally stealing a sideways glance at her husband of three hours. Adoration was written all over her face. That's always good for a marriage, Marina thought to herself.

It didn't seem so long ago that she and Jake were young and starting out. She remembered sharing dreams as they rode through the forest on that first snowy Christmas Eve. Did time always go this fast?

A series of odd noises caught her ear—the scrape of metal on metal, a deep thunk, shuffling feet, and the hint of exaggerated whispers. She listened. It was too early for anybody to be back from the basketball game.

The sharecropping house they were living in now stood at the end of a wooded lane with forests on both sides. So far, the loudest sound they'd heard out here was the nightly competition between bullfrogs and cicadas. Under the pretense of checking on the youngest ones, Marina excused herself from the table.

She glanced over at Clara, Lilli, Virginia, and Lonnie snuggled up together in a featherbed spread on the living room floor. Peering out the window into the moonless night, she could see movement down the road. As she watched, shadows formed into shapes of people. The sounds grew louder until she could distinguish pots and pans banging together. "Walt," she interrupted the conversation in the kitchen, "looks like there's going to be a shivaree."

Walt jumped up, "Sound like fun," he laughed. "Let's join 'em." He grabbed a clean pot off the stove and opened a cabinet drawer to pull out a metal soup spoon. Guiding Nora by the hand, he led his new wife through the back bedroom, easing open the window. Swinging first one leg and then the other over the sill, he dropped to the ground. Then he reached up and pulled Nora through. Marina heard her daughter-in-law giggle as they shut the window.

The mob coming up the front porch increased their racket and spilled over into the yard. So many were banging on metal it would have been difficult to decipher their words had everyone not known the demand. Shouts of laughter accompanied the clamor for the bride to be ransomed. Jake picked up the gas lamp. He, Marina, and Flora greeted the uninvited guests at the screen door. Marina recognized a few of the young people as Walt's chums from his school years.

"We want the bride and groom!" cheerful voices demanded. "They have to pay before they can play."

"You're too late!" Jake informed them. "They left."

"Let us in to look for 'em!" a burly boy cried out.

"I've got young'uns asleep in here," Jake objected. "Ya'll go on before you wake 'em up."

"Maybe Walt and Nora went to her brother's house," a platinum-haired girl suggested.

"Let's go," several of the young people shouted.

At the very back of the throng, Marina noticed two newcomers blend with the crowd. They banged the back of a pot with a large metal spoon. From her angle in the doorway, she could barely make out Walt and Nora, who had sneaked around the house to join their own shivaree. She half-smiled, thinking, "If that boy dents my cookin' pot, I'm going to blister his bottom. I don't care if he is married and livin' on his own now."

Chapter Twenty-Six

September 1940

J ake put one finger over his mouth, motioning for Marina to listen. Outside on the porch their twelve-and-a-half-year-old twins were holding a confidential powwow. Focused on her explanation, Sadie whispered louder than she intended. "Teacher said we couldn't pass to the next grade 'cause we missed too many school days last session. That wasn't our fault 'cause the danged school bus passed us right by."

"Bus passed on by 'cause we weren't at the stop when it came," Sammy responded reasonably.

"That wasn't our fault!" Sadie complained. "It came too early. I cain't get all my mornin' chores done before seven. It ought to come later."

"What are we gonna do now?" Sammy asked, confident his twin would have a plan.

"I'll fix it." Sadie dug a pencil out of her bag. "We'll promote ourselves. Give me your report card." Sammy handed it over. Sadie changed the number on front to read *Promoted to 6th Grade*. "Now I'll fix mine." She pulled out her report card and made the necessary adjustment.

"If Pappy finds out, he's gonna beat the tar out of you," Sammy predicted.

"Pappy's not gonna find out, and if he does, I'm gonna beat the tar out of you," Sadie responded with enough conviction to make Sammy a believer.

"I'm not tellin'."

"Good. Now let's get our chores done so Mommy don't suspect nothin'."

Marina shook her head. "Jake, you won't have to beat the tar out of 'em. I'll gladly do it for you. What on earth are we gonna do with those two? I tell you, I worry about that Sadie sometimes. That girl is so quick, she is always thinkin' up somethin'."

"You don't have to worry about Sadie. She's got as tender a heart as Sammy does. Her compassion will always balance out her actions. I am curious to see what they're gonna do when school starts back up. Let's hold off sayin' anything to 'em." He grinned. "You can always beat 'em later."

. . .

World demand for cotton products was down considerably that year, so it was with joy and relief that Jake announced, "Good news for Christmas!" He waved an official-looking envelope. "Our portion of the New Deal has arrived."

A smile spread over Marina's face as she looked up from the overalls she was mending. "That money will certainly come in handy," she remarked. "I didn't believe the newspaper when they announced President Roosevelt was sending checks to people who worked the land."

Jake grinned. "I know quite a few landowners that aren't as happy as we are about the provision. Clay was madder than all get out when he heard about it."

"Well, it's not his choice," Marina countered. "Landowners are gettin' their share through all the new agricultural laws congress is passin'. Some of 'em are even gettin' paid to not farm." She shook her head. "I still can't get past that. Sammy, come get these overalls. Try to be careful, son. I'm runnin' out of patches."

Marina moved to the kitchen to prepare supper. She'd picked the vegetables she needed earlier. With one smooth crack she whacked a head of iceberg lettuce against the counter so the core would pop out. At the same moment a rap on the door announced that they had a visitor.

Their landowner, Clay Barrows, stood on the other side of the screen. A thin man, about two inches taller than Jake, he wore an open jacket and a wide, striped tie. In spite of his dress clothes, Clay looked rumpled, as if discontent was spilling over his suit.

"Clay, come on in." Jake's hospitality hid his surprise. In all the years Jake had sharecropped and logged for Clay, the man had rarely visited the cabin. Jake generally went up to the owner's house to see him. "Have a seat." The children scattered to free up a chair for the adult.

"No, that won't be necessary. Jake, I've come about that Washington program and the money the federal government is mailin' out. Did you receive a check?"

"Yes, I did."

"Well, Jake, some of the other landowners and I were talkin' about it. Those men up in Washington have it all mixed up. They're not here. They don't see how it is. That check should have come to me. I'm the landowner. By rights, it's mine."

"Don't believe it is, Clay. My name's written on the check. The envelope was addressed to me."

"I'm tellin' you it's just a mix-up, Jake. You understand this is my land. I own it and I let you work it."

"Yes, you own it and I work it. This New Deal program is for those of us who work the land. That's what my family and I do."

Clay's agitation increased. "That was a mistake. Now I want you to sign that check and hand it over to me now." He held out his hand.

"That ain't gonna happen." Jake stood still, his voice even and deliberate.

"Haven't I always given you a place to live and half my cotton profits?"

"We both held to our part of the bargain. Even at fifteen years old I gave you a fair day's work for the pay. Some would say even better. The law says this money is to go to the one who works the land. That's why the check has my name on it."

"Well, you can keep the check, but you'll not work for me." Clay spit out the words, his face blotched by temper. "I want my cabin emptied on January first. Find somewhere else to live." Clay stormed out banging the screen door.

The family froze in shocked silence. The children had never heard anyone speak to their father like that before. Jake's emotions ran the gamut from anger over the injustice to hurt at being treated so badly by a man he had worked with and considered a friend to fear he had made a bad decision leaving his family without a place to live to. He turned to face his wife.

Marina's reaction was all loyalty. "The children and I will pack. You go on into town and find out who's lookin' for somebody to farm for them. They'll all be glad they finally have a chance to hire Jake Hartmann."

Assured of her support, Jake nodded at the plan. "You children help your mother," was all he said. By the time Jake had changed out of his work clothes, Roy had the mule saddled and ready.

. . .

The Hartmann family spent New Year's Day moving a few miles northwest to Buffalo Ditch. They settled into their new cabin without any discussion of what had caused the move, but the children carried with them an understanding that integrity includes an honest appreciation for your own work and the courage to ensure fairness to your family.

The new cabin was ten square feet larger. Every inch was welcome. Sammy especially loved swimming in Buffalo Ditch. He walked in dripping wet one afternoon as Marina was sweeping out the house. "Samuel Hartmann! How on earth did you get soppin' wet comin' home from school?"

"Well, I passed the ditch," Sammy began, expanding his explanation slowly. "Ever'body there was swimmin' and havin' such a good time, I figured I might as well join 'em."

"Didn't you know I'd be mad at you for swimmin' in your school clothes?"

"Yes, ma'am, but I figured you'd be madder if I swam without 'em."

Marina laughed, smacking his bottom with the broom. "Get on in there and get changed. Don't forget to bring me those clothes so I can wash 'em out and hang 'em on the line."

. . .

The season was going well. They had eighty acres to farm here in Buffalo. Mr. Bellows seemed like a decent man and landowner. Even the weather cooperated. It looked as if the harvest would bring in a good profit.

Summer days were long and hot. Most evenings saw the family migrate to the porch for lazy conversation. "Did you hear the government's restartin' the draft in October?" Roy asked.

Marina had been about to go back in the house, but stopped. "How can they do that? America's not in this war."

"First peace-time draft ever. Sounds like the good ol' USA is gearin' up to get involved. They're signin' up men ages twenty-one to thirty-six."

Virginia looked up from where she was playing on the porch. "What's a *draft*?"

"That's when they take men to be soldiers," Flora explained.

"Daddy's a soldier," Lonnie spoke up. "Was he drafted?"

"No, he signed up."

"Grandpa, will you be drafted?" Flora asked, worried.

"No, honey, I'm too old." Jake replied. "They'll be lookin' for younger men."

Clara piped up. "Will they take Walt?"

Marina frowned at the suggestion. "Probably not. They need Walter here for farmin'." She gave a hurried explanation

247

as though sweeping the possibility right off the porch. "They don't usually want to send farmers overseas."

"Roy?" Clara persisted.

"No. Everybody else is too young," Marina wanted an end to this unpleasant discussion.

Oblivious to his mother's discomfort, Hank ordered, "Well, Roy, if you do get there before me, keep that war goin' 'til I turn twenty-one."

"Let's see, when will that be?" Roy leaned back as if thinking and unable to cipher such high numbers.

"August 1, 1946." Hank had already done his calculations.

Absorbed in their conversation, the family didn't notice Mr. Bellows coming down the path until he was almost to the porch. "Jake, Marina, how y'all doin' this evenin'?" Norm Bellows was a broad, bulky man with a twiggy moustache and a silky voice.

"Fine, thank you. Come on up, Mr. Bellows. Sit a spell."

Mr. Bellows mounted the steps, settling into the rocker Hank quickly vacated. "I heard y'all talkin' 'bout the draft as I was walkin' up. It's good that none of your boys will be called."

"Doesn't look like it unless the war lasts a lot longer than everyone's predictin'," Jake agreed.

Mr. Bellows nodded. "As you were sayin', since Walt is farmin', it's not likely he'll be called up. My boy Louis is about your Walt's age. In fact, that's why I'm here. On the day they institute the draft, I'd like him to have that same protection as your boy Walt. I need to put him here, farmin' this eighty. Sorry

248

about this, Jake. You're a good man. I like your family. I hate that it's come to this, but I can't take a chance on losin' my boy in the war. You understand."

Jake understood alright. He understood he wasn't a landowner. He looked Mr. Bellows in the eye and asked, "When would you like us to move out?"

"Oh, no hurry," Mr. Bellows waved a massive hand as if dismissing the details. "Just so's my boy can be in charge before the end of the month." He stood up, surprisingly agile for a man of his size. Walking down the steps, he turned around for one last comment. "You might want to talk to Oliver Rankin across the road here. He's older and his back's been givin' him some trouble. Chances are he'd be pleased to have someone sharecrop for him, especially someone like you. I'd be happy to give you a reference. Y'all have a good night now."

Chapter Twenty-Seven

November 1940

"**M**ommy." As usual Sadie took the initiative to speak for both twins. "Sammy and I wanna go over here to School Sixteen instead of ridin' the bus into Leachville." Marina stirred the pork fat liquefying on the stove. So this was how the rascals planned to get by with having changed their report cards to read *Promoted to 6ᵗʰ Grade*. They aimed to change schools.

She glanced at Jake, who was pulling on his boots, readying to go to the fields. His expression remained deadpanned, but she knew that face well. He seemed almost proud of the children for figuring out a solution to the mess they had put themselves in. Bigger Rascal! Clearly, they got it from his side.

"Wouldn't you rather ride the bus instead of walkin'?" Marina questioned as she poured rendered fat through a steel colander, straining out the gristle.

The twins exchanged anxious looks.

"No, ma'am. We like to walk—good exercise," Sadie replied. Marina kept silent, avoiding the obvious question of when had a sharecropper's child ever needed more exercise.

"How will they know which grade you're in?" she asked, feigning innocence. Jake shot her a quick look. Most people would not suspect his wife had a little orneriness of her own.

"Oh, we have our report cards from last year."

Sammy spoke up. "If we walk to School Sixteen, you won't have to worry 'bout us missin' the school bus to Manila."

"There is that," she conceded. "Alright, you best get walkin' then."

The next morning after breakfast, Marina pulled out her soap molds, lye, the rainwater she'd been collecting, and the fat she'd rendered the day before. Sadie came into the kitchen with her school books. "Mommy, did you know your cousin, Mr. Amerson, is principal here at Sixteen?"

"Oh, yes." Marina responded. "He's been principal here for five or six years."

"You seen him lately?" Sadie asked, shifting from one foot to the next.

"No, not lately." Truth was she hadn't seen him for a couple of years, but it wouldn't hurt Sadie to worry a little about the possibility her mother and the principal might be communicating. "Did he say hello to you yesterday?"

Sadie nodded. "He was standin' out in front of the school building when we got there. We sure were surprised to see him."

Marina nodded as she dissolved lye into cold rainwater, stirring it with a wooden spoon. "I imagine you were. What did he have to say?"

"Nothin' much. He asked us what grade we're in. We told him sixth and he said, 'Okay, go on in and sit on the left side.' So we did." Sadie waited, knowing her mother needed to focus while she combined heated lard with the lye mixture. When Marina began stirring again, Sadie repeated, "You sure you ain't talked to him lately?"

"No, I haven't. Now you and Sammy better get goin' or you'll be late to school." Relieved, Sadie started out the door. "Oh, and Sadie...." The girl paused and Marina continued, "Be sure to tell my cousin Kyle I said hello. We need to get together some time."

"Yes, ma'am." Deflated, Sadie continued outside.

Jake laughed, shaking his head at his wife before heading outside.

Smiling, Marina continued to stir for another thirty minutes. When the liquid reached a consistency like honey, she poured the mixture into rectangular wooden molds lined with cotton cloth cut from flour sacks. Wrapping them in towels, she set the soap boxes out of the way on the kitchen hutch to cure.

That school year proved to be the longest of the twins' education. They had missed so many days of instruction the previous year that they struggled to keep pace in class. Every night Sadie and Sammy brought home books and studied until Jake commanded lights out. Their lives consisted of nothing more than school, chores, homework, and an occasional dip in Buffalo Ditch. "They're payin' for their mischief," Jake grinned.

"Good thing they're smart enough to do two years of schoolin' in one," Marina agreed.

.   .   .

"Sammy got over that fever and sore throat a couple weeks ago and now he has a rash on his trunk and legs," Marina commented. "At first, I thought it might be somethin' he picked up swimmin' but now I don't think so."

"Do you think he's coming down with the measles?" Jake asked, concerned.

"That's not a measles rash. He says his stomach hurts. The fever's come back. Sammy's never been one to complain, but you can tell he's miserable."

Sammy continued to weaken over the next several days. Marina noticed he was swelling. His joints were red and hot. Soon his muscles were so weak he wasn't able to walk or hold a book to read. Jake read the panic in Marina's eyes and sent for the doctor.

Old Doc Franklin examined the boy and shook his head. "I don't know what it is. Let him rest and make sure he eats something. Maybe it'll run its course."

The swelling increased, leaving Sammy almost immobile. He lay on the sofa, too weak to hold a book. His brothers and sisters tried to coax, cajole, and, in the case of Sadie, threaten, him into getting better, but nothing worked. This was one time sweet, gentle-hearted, accommodating Sammy could not comply.

Mr. Millstead, who sharecropped the next forty acres over, stopped by to visit. When he saw Sammy was no longer able to sit up, he mentioned his brother's wife had been cured by a doctor in Paragould. Jake and Marina took the day off work, leaving the older children in charge of the fields and animals, and made the journey with Sammy. Like everything else they had tried, the thirty-mile trip was fruitless. The Paragould doctor admitted he had never seen anything like it.

Cotton season started. Marina felt torn. She needed to get back out in the fields again, but she couldn't stand the thought of leaving Sammy alone in the cabin. She studied on it while preparing supper. They really couldn't afford to leave Flora, Sadie, or Emily at the house with him. They needed the girls to hoe. They were already missing Sammy's contribution. Finally she came up with a plan.

After they ate, she heated a big pot of water, announcing, "Girls, clean up the kitchen and set some beans to soakin' for tomorrow's dinner." Then she disappeared outside with the

254

pot. She dumped the hot water into a bucket. Next, she selected a chicken and wrung its neck. Holding the dead hen by its feet, she plunged it up and down in the water for about thirty seconds to loosen the feathers. With experienced fingers she plucked quickly, stuffing the feathers into a burlap bag from the barn. Feathers from this hen, along with the others she had been saving, would be just enough for what she had in mind.

Back inside, she folded a remnant of tick, the blue-and-white-striped cotton cloth she used for covering mattresses. She cut out a long rectangle and sewed up the sides. Turning the five-and-a-half-foot pouch right side out, she began stuffing it with chicken feathers. When it was completely full, she sewed up the opening. "That'll do fine," she commented, satisfied.

The next morning after breakfast she asked Roy to bring the wagon around. "Are you takin' Sammy to a new doctor?" he asked.

"No, I'm takin' him to the fields so I can hoe cotton."

Jake picked up Sammy's weakened twelve-year old body, carefully placing him on the long pillow Marina had made the night before. It was just a little bit longer than the boy was tall. Then Jake picked up the pillow with Sammy on it and carried him out to the wagon. Sadie scrambled in beside him, anxiously watching her brother's every move.

"She'd take the illness for him if she could," Jake murmured.

Marina nodded. "I would too."

255

Bumps and divots along the lane made for a rough journey to the fields. Jake set his son on the pillow under the wagon shade so the sun couldn't beat on him while they worked. Each member of the family then scattered to their rows. Marina hoed on the ends so she could keep a close eye on Sammy. At lunchtime, she sat on her cotton sack, coaxing a little water between his lips so he wouldn't get overheated.

Hoeing time melted into harvest, but Sammy did not improve. The family continued transporting him in the wagon. Neighbors and relatives suggested homemade remedies. Marina tried them all. Nothing worked.

One Sunday afternoon, Marina's brother Wade and his family stopped in to visit. Unable to sit up at the table with everyone else for dinner, Sammy remained on his giant pillow in the living room. "I've heard about a doctor up in Hornersville, Missouri," Wade began haltingly. He knew it was expensive to take someone to one doctor after another. "I know ya'll have been to a lot of 'em already." He paused to look over at Sammy before continuing. "They say this doctor's real good. He used to do some kind of research at one of them universities." Wade paused again, afraid to give his sister too much encouragement. "I guess maybe he's seen more than some of our doctors 'round here. He's supposed to be real smart, knows about some of them new medicines that have been discovered."

Marina stared at her brother, soaking in every word. Jake nodded. "We'll take him."

The trip north was a bumpy one. Sammy lay in the back of the wagon on a full-sized feather mattress surrounded by pillows. All the way to Hornersville, Marina kept turning around to check on him.

The doctor's office overflowed with patients, which they took to be evidence this physician was better than most. After a two-and-a-half-hour wait, the nurse ushered them into the examination room. Jake gently placed his son on the table.

Dr. Bond was a small-boned man in his late forties with hair beginning to silver around the temples and thin over the crown. Marina had never met anyone who listened so intently. He collected information, asking questions to clarify the symptoms and identify which remedies had been tried.

When Marina finished her narrative, he nodded, made a few more notes, and then began his examination. He glanced over the rash, not seeming to give it much attention. He lifted Sammy's arms and legs, scrutinizing each joint, apologizing for the pain he knew he was causing. Placing his stethoscope against Sammy's chest, he listened intently for several minutes. That was the only time Marina saw him frown. He finished the examination and then sat down behind his desk.

"He starts to get better, then all of a sudden he'll take a turn for the worse and we don't know why," Marina explained. "We don't know what we're doin' to make it worse."

"It's nothing you're doing. It's the nature of the illness. It always comes and goes like this."

257

"You've seen this before then?" Jake clarified.

Doctor Bond nodded. "Two times."

"Can you do anything for him?"

The doctor stood up. At first, Marina thought they were being dismissed, that he was saying there was no hope. Without a word, he pulled a key out of his pocket and unlocked a cabinet above his desk. He reached in, pulling out a small tin which he handed to them. "Here. Take this powder. Dissolve it in salt water. I don't know what it is your son has, but if you give him this and he has complete rest, he'll eventually get better.

Jake looked at the tin holding the powder. "What kind of medicine is this?" he asked, curious.

Dr. Bond hesitated. "It's something we've been working with in the lab at the university. We don't know why it works, but it does. I've seen good results with several types of infections. I'm going to show you how to mix it up and I'll write out the directions too. He needs to take this medicine until it's gone. Samuel needs to continue on complete rest even after he's feeling better. No running or rough-housing for a full year. Now I mean that. Nothing! Any activity at all will make him worse. No wrestling for three or four years."

The doctor gave Sammy his first dose. Turning back to Marina, he patted her on the shoulder. "You did the right thing in coming to me."

A few physicians like Dr. Bond were beginning to identify the symptoms of rheumatic fever and recognize the curative powers of penicillin. The advent of another world war would kick production into high gear so that the medicine would become available in drug stores.

Marina's heart felt more freedom on the wagon trip home than it had in months. Sammy still lay immobile in the back, but Marina's hope for her son's healing had matured into faith.

Chapter Twenty-Eight

December 1941

Over four thousand miles away the Japanese bombed Pearl Harbor. Without warning, Marina's life in Mississippi County, Arkansas, changed. Goods were rationed. Fear of the draft set in. The war tainted everything. Outwardly, Marina continued working, while inwardly, she held herself tight. Some mothers were saying goodbye to their sons forever. She had no guarantee she wouldn't be one of them.

Rosa Lee went to work in a munitions factory. Who could have ever imagined sweet, gentle Rosa Lee manufacturing bullets, but she did it with the same cheerfulness she used to meet every challenge. Six months later, Emily's sweetheart, John, was drafted. Roy signed up in '42.

In November of 1942, the government expanded the draft to include all men ages eighteen to thirty-seven. That fit right in with Hank's tactics to win the war. The army cooperated with his plan even further by drafting the boy shortly after he turned eighteen the following August. They put Hank on a ship headed for the Philippines.

.   .   .

"Lilli, help me get this table cleared. Sammy, go turn on the radio and see if you can get a clear signal. It's almost time for the broadcast. Maybe we'll hear something about Hank's ship. So much of his last letter was blacked out, it hardly made sense."

"Granny, I know the name of Uncle Hank's ship," Lonnie announced. "It's the U.S.S. Benjamin Jordan!"

"That's right."

"My daddy's not on a ship. He's all the way over in Saudee Arabie, right?" Lonnie questioned.

"That's right. Now you go throw these scraps to the chickens, then come on in and get ready to listen."

Emily washed the dishes while Sadie dried. Lilli finished wiping down the table. Clara wrapped the leftover food securely, storing it in the ice box. Virginia helped by putting the salt shaker away in its place on the kitchen hutch. Smiling, Marina picked up the broom and began to sweep. She'd never tell them, but she thought her girls were wonderful. She didn't have a lazy one in the bunch.

Static blared from the radio as Sammy adjusted the knobs. Marina's heart always beat a little faster until they caught a clear signal. Even though she didn't recognize the names of most of the cities and even some of the countries the newscaster listed, this radio broadcast was still the closest she could get to hearing news about Roy and Hank.

"I think I've got it," Sammy called. The Glenn Miller Band blared out "In the Mood." Done with chores, Sadie danced her way from the clean kitchen to the living room, laughing as she stepped past Pappy, who had already settled into his rocker.

"The jitterbug!" Lilli cried. "Teach me to do it, Sadie." Catching the rhythm, Lilli followed about a half a step behind her sister's lead. Right foot, side step. Left foot, side step. Right foot, back of the left heel. Left foot, step in place.

Eyes sparkling and black hair flying, Sadie grabbed her sister's hand, swinging her under to the left. Lilli lost her balance and almost ended up on top of Pappy, who laughed, shaking his head at their nonsense. The song ended with a musical flourish, and both out-of-breath girls collapsed on the sofa.

"Ya'll come on," Marina called. "It's about time for the show to start."

"I think the show's already started," Jake nodded toward the giggling girls.

Marina sat down in her rocker. Virginia, already settled on the floor, then scooted over next to her. The announcer spoke, and it was as if the sound of his words caused the voices of the family to click off.

"The News of the World, Thursday, February 3rd. Once again Columbia and world capitals and fighting zones of the western Pacific are ready to give you the latest news direct by shortwave radio."

The sound of the broadcaster's voice broke off. Static increased. For a moment, Marina thought the radio had lost its signal. She was about to say something to Sammy when the announcer's voice came back. "I'm sorry, folks. This just off the wire. . . .I'm afraid it's not good news. The transporter the U.S.S. Benjamin Jordan, sailing at an undisclosed location in the Pacific, has been torpedoed. The ship sank. We don't have a list of names yet, but it is believed there are no survivors. Again, the transporter the U.S.S. Benjamin Jordan, sailing at an undisclosed location in the Pacific, has been torpedoed. The ship has sunk. It is believed there are no survivors. We'll update you more as we receive further information."

"Sammy, turn it off," Jake commanded, his anguish coming out in harsh tones.

The radio snapped off. No one moved. The silence deepened. Although the room had been quiet while they listened, the lack of conversation had felt normal. This awkward silence cut sharp, stifling the breath, stabbing the heart.

Finally, Lonnie broke the noiselessness. "Did Uncle Hank's ship blow up, Grandpa?"

"No!" Marina answered before anyone else could. "He wasn't on that ship."

"They said the U.S.S. Benjamin Jordan," Lonnie reminded her.

"He wasn't on that ship," Marina repeated. "He was. . .somewhere else."

"You kids get ready for bed," Jake instructed.

Marina grabbed a wash bucket and headed out into the dark night. The frosty night air rushed over her face, stinging her flushed cheeks.

"Mommy, you forgot your coat," she heard Clara cry.

"Leave her be," Jake's voice answered. "She doesn't need it tonight."

Marina sat the wash bucket down in front of the pump. Grabbing the cold metal, she jerked the handle up and down, priming the pump with such a vengeance that water soon gushed from the spout, flowing over the top of the bucket. She wanted to scream into the night, but knew that if she did, she would be accepting the newscaster's words.

She pumped and pumped and wished she could go on pumping until she had filled a thousand buckets. Needing to keep moving, she walked around the yard, frustrated there was no way to work out her whole mishmash of feelings. Finally, she returned to the pump, jerking the bucket up and spilling a third of the water back onto the splash block.

The children were all in bed when she entered the house. Marina knew she should go to the older ones, who must be lying there awake, but she couldn't bring herself to do it. To comfort someone is to acknowledge a loss.

Dipping her scrub brush into the soapy water, she attacked the floor with a ferocity that could have taken out a squadron of Axis forces. The whishing noise of the bristles broke the calm. She scrubbed the floor over and over, scouring the already clean boards long into the night.

Morning crawled slowly to life. Way before time to rise, the smell of fried eggs popping in bacon grease filled the house. Marina cooked with the speed of an aching heart in need of movement. Platters of bacon, pitchers of fresh milk, a pint jar of grape jelly, and stacks of biscuits filled the table. Her hands slapped dishes on the table with a determination that challenged anyone to disrupt the normalcy she was insisting on. The older girls knew to stay out of their mother's way, focusing instead on helping the little ones. The family would be in the fields early today.

"Pappy, what about Hank," she heard Lilli ask softly.

"We don't know anything yet," Jake's voice carried across the room with an assurance that calmed his children's hearts. "The government will notify us if there is something to tell. Our job is to take care of business here at home."

"Breakfast is ready! Get in here before it gets cold," Marina called.

Night crept in again, still no news. Marina slipped into bed beside Jake, her head on his shoulder. "He wasn't on that ship," she insisted. "I would know if he was. . .gone. I would feel it."

Jake held her tighter. He thought back on years of watching her read the hearts of their children. She had an uncanny sense of knowing when they were sad or needed to talk or were just plain guilty about something. The children always complained they could never hide anything from their mother. Jake kissed the top of her head. "Then there's no reason for us to give in to fear, is there?" he asked. It was more of a statement than a question.

Love for this strong man of hers flooded Marina's heart, and a calm assurance took possession of her mind. "No," she agreed, snuggling in closer. "No reason at all."

Those were slow but productive days on the farm. The Hartmanns all focused on their tasks, and when they didn't have chores to do, they invented new ones to keep busy. It was almost as though the harder they worked, the more strength they possessed to push away any danger to the life they had so painstakingly cultivated. The physical efforts of work provided a layer of protection from the worrisome pricks of imagination.

Still no word. Each new morning brought a greater cushion of comfort. Then the telegram came.

It was midday and Marina was preparing dinner. Knowing the others would be home in about thirty minutes, she hurried to have everything ready. She emptied a quart jar of corn into a pot, tossing in a little salt, some of her fresh butter, and a spoonful of sugar. She gave the pot a stir, then checked to see how the chicken pot pie was browning. She began slicing the loaves of bread she had baked that morning.

The door opened, and Marina spun around, wondering if she had misjudged the time. Jake stood there. Just him, without the children. He didn't say anything. Her eyes traveled down his arm to the envelope he held at his side. It was torn open. Even at this distance, she could see the government seal.

She stood there, not taking the envelope from him. It wouldn't be true until she read it.

Jake began to shake his head. "Hank was on the boat. The torpedo blast threw him into the water. That saved his life. He's hurt. He's hurt badly and may lose his leg. He'll be in the hospital for a long time. Then he'll come home. He'll come home," Jake repeated.

Marina threw herself into his arms, sobbing all her dammed up tears.

Sunday arrived and with it gratitude for a place to express a heart rich with thanksgiving. The old church stood a little over a mile from where they were living now. The folks who lived the farthest away started walking first. Then as they passed a house, the family who lived there would come out and join the walk. Soon there was a throng of church-goers.

Each family congratulated them on the news that Hank had survived the torpedoing. She thanked them all, especially Roland Sorrells, who had brought the telegram from town.

Over thirty neighbors joined the stroll, children racing, beaus teasing, and women chatting.

The sun shone brighter than on most February days. They were almost to the crossroads when the sound of moaning interrupted their conversations. It wasn't crying exactly, more like a fretful complaint intermittent with blasts of wails piercing the words. Clara and Virginia skipped ahead to discover what was going on.

Just as the family reached the edge of the church grounds, the girls were back. "It's Miz Cox. Her son's been drafted," they announced.

"Did he leave for camp already?" Emily asked.

"Nope. He's up at the church too. He's got another month to go before he leaves," Clara answered.

Sadie scoffed. "Don't know why in the world she's carrying on like that. He's not even over there yet." A stern look from her mother encouraged Sadie to withdraw to a group of her friends.

Polly Patrice Cox was a widow now. Her husband had died three years before. Upon hearing the news, Hank had commented it was probably the only way the poor man could get any rest from that wife of his. Marina had chided him for such an uncharitable comment, but not with too much enthusiasm. After all, children shouldn't be discouraged from telling the truth.

Right now her attention focused on the woman in front of her. Marina understood the fear that grabs a mother's heart when her son gets called up. Polly Patrice Cox may never have been a close friend, but now Marina regarded her with pure compassion. That woman had a lot of sleepless nights ahead of her.

Marina spoke a few comforting words before starting up the church steps. Behind her a crowd of women surrounded Polly Patrice, each commiserating and offering a pat on the arm. All the sympathy seemed to make the situation worse, encouraging Polly Patrice to wail even louder. "What will I do? What will become of me? My husband's dead. My daughters are married and livin' in Leachville. Now my only son is leavin' me to go get hisself killed. What will become of me? Who will take care of me?"

Miz Pearl McDowell pushed her way through the crowd. Four-foot-eleven inches with white curly hair, she looked far too frail to be the mother of twelve children. "Polly Patrice," she instructed in a stern voice. "You've got to be strong. That boy of yours is over yonder by the water pump, and he can hear ever' word yer sayin'. You don't want to send him off to fight with those words of death ringin' in his ears. A mother's job is to be strong for her children. Let that boy of yours know you believe he can do it. Let him know yer proud he's doin' his duty." In a voice that had brooked no nonsense from her well-over-six-foot sons, Pearl McDowell now instructed Polly Patrice, "Tell him he's *not* to get killed. Remind him you'll be needin' him at home after he's won the war."

Polly Patrice looked at Pearl with disdain. "That's all well and good for you. You have seven sons and three daughters, ever' one of 'em livin' right here in Manila. It wouldn't matter so much to you if one of your boys got killed. But what's to become of me?"

A collective intake of breath froze the moment like a stalled picture show.

Pearl McDowell drew back her arm, and in a punch that would have made any one of her seven sons proud, knocked Polly Patrice right back into her crowd of sympathizers.

The crowd gasped and Pearl McDowell calmly continued up the church steps. Just before the open door, her eyes met Marina's and locked. They stood there for a moment, two mothers, each understanding the other. Then Marina took a step back and motioned toward the church. "After you, Miz McDowell."

Chapter Twenty-Nine

October 1943

Emily sat in shocked silence, her hand still holding the open letter.

"What's the matter?" Sadie asked, plopping down beside her sister. The sharpness of Sadie's tone caught Marina's attention. She turned around from the pork chops she was frying to listen.

"It's John."

"Well, you're holdin' a letter from him, and his parents haven't received any telegrams, so he must be alright," Sadie responded practically. "What does he say?"

"The Germans shot down his plane." Emily fought back the tears. Marina turned off the flame below the meat and joined them to listen.

"His letter says they kept the plane goin' until it drifted into Switzerland. John and his crew have been captured by the

Swiss. The army blacked out the rest of the letter." Emily looked miserable.

Marina frowned. "I thought the Swiss were supposed to be neutral."

"To them neutral just means they're not for or against either side. They won't help the Allies or Axis. If a plane crashes within their territory, the Swiss government interns the crew."

"What does that mean, *interns*?" Sadie asked.

"John's a prisoner." Emily's voice trembled.

Marina felt helpless. She didn't know how to comfort her daughter or what to say. Sadie, never hampered by indecisiveness, took charge.

"Don't you worry," she commanded. "So what if the army blacked out half of his letter. He let you know where he is — well, at least that he's somewhere in Switzerland. He's alive and the important thing is he's thinkin' about you. You listen to me, Emily. John has been in love with you since you were fifteen years old, and he'll be in love with you when you're ninety. You just hold on. When this war is over, he'll find his way home to you. Not even the Nazis can keep John Wallis from coming home and marryin' you."

Unsure of what to say, Marina patted her daughter's shoulder. Her heart ached for her girl. She couldn't imagine losing Jake.

Sadie continued. "This is not a German prison. It's a Swiss internment. Did John give an address where you can write him?"

Emily nodded.

"Alright, then. You get busy. You send him a letter ever' day until he comes home. It'll be alright."

Obeying her confident, younger sister, Emily secured pen and paper and began to write.

Marina went back to cooking pork chops. Her children's skills always amazed her. How had Sadie known exactly the right thing to say?

The next several weeks passed, highlighted by occasional news from overseas. John wrote about prisoners who tried to escape. The lines revealing what happened to the men had been blacked out. Emily kept a brave face and planned their future.

The family kept two cows now—one a Jersey, the other a Holstein. After breakfast, Marina began the process of churning her weekly butter. "That's clotting nicely," she commented to Sammy, who was helping. She looked up and noticed the watchful faces of Lilli, Clara, Virginia, and Lonnie all holding tin cups, patiently waiting for the sweet cream buttermilk. She laughed and filled their cups.

Next, Marina poured the butter into a bowl and beat it with a wooden spoon to rid it of water. Once that was done, she packed butter into her round mold. "I believe we'll get three pounds out of this—one for Mrs. Flinnett, one for our family to eat, and one to sell in town on Saturday. Butter's sellin' for ten cents a pound."

"Mommy, why do you always give Mrs. Flinnett a pound of our butter?" Clara questioned.

"Clara, we have enough for our family and plenty leftover to sell. We can afford to give to someone who is goin' without." Feeling a bit chastised, Clara nodded.

The butter turned out beautifully. Marina took pride in the clear, yellow color. Her mold's round shape was crowned by a rose. "That'll do just fine," she approved.

On Saturday, their wagon pulled up in front of Mrs. Flinnett's unpainted clapboard house. Half-a-dozen skinny children played in the dirt, looking up with interest as Marina approached the bungalow.

Marina knocked. Although the door was open, no one appeared. The children continued to watch, but no one offered to go get their mother. After waiting a full minute, she knocked again. "Mrs. Flinnett," she called through the broken screen.

She heard the scrape of a chair on wood, and a stalky-looking woman with a sharp face ambled into the room, looking a bit perturbed at the interruption. The woman's greedy eyes went immediately to the cloth-covered butter Marina was holding. "Oh, it's you, Mrs. Hartmann."

"Yes. How are you? We were comin' to town and I thought I would stop by with some butter." Marina lifted the cloth to allow the woman a peek.

Mrs. Flinnett frowned but took the butter, albeit a little reluctantly. Marina wondered if the woman was embarrassed by the gift. Strange, she had never seemed uncomfortable before, and Marina had been bringing her a weekly gift of butter for several months now.

The woman twisted her mouth without making a sound, and then in a high-pitched voice said, "Mrs. Hartmann, my sister buys her butter in a rectangular shape. I prefer mine that way too. Do you think next time you could shape mine into a rectangle?"

Marina was dumb-founded, but responded in measured tones, "No, I don't believe I can. I have a round butter mold. You'll be able to find someone who does and you can buy your butter from her." Resisting the urge to grab her butter back, she forced a smile and returned to her family waiting in the wagon. Next week, she thought, we'll have two pounds of butter to sell in town.

. . .

Roy was discharged in time to help with the choppin'. He came home and resumed chores. It was almost as though he picked up the hoe he had just laid down. As was typical of him, he kept his own counsel, never talking about his time in the army. Marina, however, flew around the house, overflowing with her share of happiness and his too.

A letter written by one of Hank's nurses arrived a few days later. Marina paused beside the curtained doorway of the bedroom to reread a paragraph. He might be shipped home within six months. As she read, she was distracted by the sound of Lilli whispering. "Don't tell." The words piqued Marina's curiosity and she listened.

"We think Mommy's hidin' oranges," Lilli explained.

"We smelled 'em," Clara's voice confirmed. Marina peeked past the curtain edge to see who was participating in the conversation. Clara and Lilli were talking to Virginia.

"We think she's keeping the oranges for Christmas, but we don't want to wait that long."

"We've been huntin' for 'em," Clara bragged.

"We 'specially don't want the boys to find 'em. They'd gobble 'em all up before we could get a bite."

Virginia nodded agreement as Lilli continued. "We've looked in the pantry, in the wardrobe, even under the bed. No luck so far, but we're not givin' up."

"No, sir!" Clara"s insisted.

"Soon as Mommy goes out to the hen house, we're gonna go look in the root cellar."

"Those little hooligans!" Marina thought. She stepped away from the curtain. "Girls!"

Lilli, Clara, and Virginia appeared from behind the curtain with guilty expressions on their sweet faces.

"I need you to run some of Great-Aunt Diana's sweet pickles down the road to Mrs. Vassar. Go get a jar out of the cellar and scoot on over to her house. All three of you can go."

Lilli shot Clara a coy smile. "Yes, ma'am. We're happy to do it."

Marina turned away so the girls couldn't see her smile. "All right then. Go on."

The girls shot out the door without another word.

Marina busied herself in the house, dusting items on her knick-knack shelf and slicing potatoes for frying.

Finally, they emerged with a jar of pickles, but looking dejected. Marina almost felt guilty herself. She waited until the girls were well down the road before retrieving a sack of oranges from behind the kitchen hutch and hiding them in the cellar where the girls had just searched. "Now we'll see if they think to look twice in the same spot," she challenged.

Over the next several days the girls continued their hunt. They searched the dish cabinets, the pie safe, even inside an old traveling trunk, anywhere they thought they could safely access without being seen by their mother. Marina stayed one step behind them, always hiding the oranges wherever the girls had just looked. Moving the oranges around from place to place left a hint of citrus in the air and drove the girls to even greater distraction.

On Christmas Eve, Marina sent the children out to ice skate on the flooded, frozen pasture so she could spend a quiet afternoon baking. She set the flour, salt, eggs, sugar, lard, milk, and baking powder out on the kitchen counter. She was in the process of separating the eggs when an idea suddenly occurred to her. Chuckling to herself, she pulled an orange out of the traveling trunk where it was currently hidden. She zested the fruit, dumping the shredded peelings on top of the flour. Then she substituted the orange's juice for some of the cream. "We'll see how this turns out," she laughed.

By the time the children came in from the pasture, the coconut cake was frosted, wrapped, and untouchable until Christmas dinner. "I'm going to be sad when the water in the pasture melts and we can't skate anymore," Virginia sighed.

"Maybe we'll get a lot of rain in the spring and we can go boatin' in the tub again," Lilli encouraged.

"Not too much rain." Marina added her wishes.

Sammy spoke up. "Mommy, before mornin' you might find a ghost has cut hisself a slice of your beautiful coconut cake."

"That ghost might find himself with a tanned hide too," Marina responded.

"Gotta catch him first," Sammy grinned and was out the door to tend the animals.

"Walk! Doctor said no runnin'!" Marina called after him. Except for still tiring easily, Sammy looked as though he was almost back to normal. What a relief to have to scold him for being too active!

"I smell an orange," Clara announced. Evidently her patience had worn out.

"You must be dreamin' and walkin' in your sleep," Marina responded. "Go get your evenin' chores done."

278

The girls obeyed reluctantly. "Bet she's been eatin' 'em herself," Lilli grumbled just loud enough for her mother to hear.

Christmas morning dawned with a clarity that underlined its purpose. The children were up early, whistling their way through chores. Even though the Hartmanns did not exchange gifts, the day still felt like a celebration. Only essential chores were required. They'd have plenty of time for playing.

Before noon they had all the work done and had cleaned up at the pump. Marina set the table, placing a brightly scrubbed orange in the middle of each plate.

"You did have oranges!" the girls cried. "Where were you hiding them?"

"Oh, I don't tell my secrets!" Marina laughed.

The girls cleared the table from the main meal and Marina brought in the coconut cake. She watched closely as they took a bite their faces registering shock. "Orange! You put orange in the coconut cake!" Marina chuckled to herself about that all evening.

New Year's Day came with confidence that the war was about to end and life would be normal again. The little information she could gather when a nurse took a few minutes to write a letter for Hank assured her that he was improving steadily. She ached to get him home where she could get her hands on him. As always, she focused on her daily tasks, letting the weeks and months take care of themselves.

. . .

"Sammy, would you cut me some splints out of this pasteboard? The girls are going to need new sunbonnets when it comes time for choppin'." Sammy complied and Marina began sewing the material. She created a ruffle to keep the splint from falling out.

"Mommy, can't we do without the bonnets this year?" Clara complained. "They're so hot. It's hard to see beyond the ruffle, and besides, they aren't in style anymore."

"Burnt red faces aren't in style either. You'll be glad you have a bonnet when you look in the mirror and see your face isn't tanned."

Spring came on. With more joy than even the end of the war would bring her, Marina welcomed her son home. She and the girls fussed over Hank, putting pillows behind his back and under his leg. She couldn't do enough to satisfy her own desire to serve him.

Emily wrote John faithfully. Letters flew back and forth across mountains and ocean as they made their plans. She even sent him a thirty-dollar cablegram once. Word was that he would be released sometime after the war ended. Then his letters stopped. No warning, no explanation. They simply stopped coming.

Emily continued to write. She didn't appear worried, but she moved at a faster pace and shared her thoughts less often.

The family exchanged looks, but no one voiced any fears. His parents had not received any notice. If John was alive, he would find his way back to Emily.

Then one afternoon, John appeared at the office where Emily worked. He had escaped over the mountains into French Allied territory where he was able to ride an army plane back to the states. There were no soles left on his shoes, and he swore he'd never leave Arkansas again. Five days later, his parents drove John and Emily to the same courthouse where Marina and Jake had married thirty-two years before.

The summer solstice was hot that year. After supper, the family naturally gravitated to the front porch. Adults settled into the rockers, pulling out extra chairs from inside. The youngsters perched wherever they could find a roost.

A slight breeze swept across the delta, stirring Marina's flowers and intoxicating the twilight. Katydids shook their legs in rhythm. Night crickets added a one-note cadence. The ancient bull frog chorus sang especially loudly. In amongst them lightning bugs flitted, reminding everyone of childhood freedoms they had almost forgotten. Story telling was inevitable.

"There's a man out at Milligan Ridge been livin' in a tree for years. . . ." Sammy tossed the words out, then waited patiently for someone to question him.

"How can you live in a tree?" Lonnie asked, fascinated and thinking that might be a good move for him when he got older.

"Oh, those are big old trees. Some of 'em hundreds of years old—big around, maybe twelve feet across." Sammy nodded. "Yep, that old man made himself a nice-sized room. Looked like lightnin' had chopped off the top of that tree. The old man cut it down to where it's only seven or eight feet tall now. He burned out the insides so's it would be hollow and moved in."

"Does it snow on him?" Lonnie asked.

"Naw, he put planks over the top to make a sort of roof."

"Are you foolin' me, Uncle Sammy?" Lonnie asked, doubtful.

Sammy smiled gently. "No, sir. I've seen it."

"Even with a roof, how does he stay warm enough? How does he cook?" Sadie questioned. "If he lit a fire, he'd suffocate himself."

"He took care of that. Stove pipe comes right out of the top of the stump."

"Doesn't sound like a very pleasant place to live." Emily was thinking about the coziness of the rock house where she and John had recently set up housekeeping.

"I guess it suits him."

Lonnie couldn't hold his excitement any longer. "I'd sure like to live out there with him."

"You 'bout as well stay right here at home," Flora advised her son.

"Yes, sir. That's the truth of it," Hank agreed. "Ain't nothin' better than what we've got right here."

"Is your leg comfortable?" Marina questioned. He had it propped on an upside-down crate with a feather pillow in between for softening.

"My leg's comfortable enough as long as it's still attached to my middle and goes all the way to the floor. Those blasted doctors wanted to cut my leg clean off. I told 'em no, but they were insistin'!"

"How'd you get 'em to leave you alone?" Sadie asked.

"First doctor said, 'We need to amputate that leg.' I told him, 'No, sir, you will not.' He left and came back with two more just like him. They said, 'We're sorry, but we're going to cut off your leg.' They were gonna do it too. They were comin' right toward me. I grabbed hold of that bed rail and swung myself sideways. Then I pulled myself to my feet and yelled, 'You son of a. . . .'" Hank paused, glanced at his mother, and did a bit of on-the-spot editing. "'You son of a gun! You ain't touchin' my leg. I'll get a gun and blow your head off.' Then I looked around at all the other soldiers in that hospital ward and hollered, 'Men, are you with me?' And to a one they stood and yelled, 'We are with you.' Those doctors backed out of that ward and never bothered me no more." Hank patted his leg.

Everyone looked at the rescued leg. For a moment the story-telling ceased while the cicadas gossiped about the toughness of Arkansas boys.

"Well, it's good to have you boys home," Jake commented.

"It sure is," Emily agreed, glancing up at her handsome husband with pride. "I began to think you were never going to get home."

Walt spoke up. "I never did hear the story of how you ended up in Switzerland, John."

Not a big talker, John hesitated before answering. "We'd completed our mission and were on our way back. A green-and-blue German Messerschmitt dropped out of the clouds. I thought we'd be able to outrun him, but he hit us. Phil, our pilot, kept us steady until we coasted into neutral territory. I gave the order and the team lined up. First man jumped. Next man waited to make sure the man's parachute had opened, and then he jumped. They followed one right after the other. It was down to the last guy. He stood at the door of the plane refusing to move. I yelled at him to jump, but he just stood there."

"Was he afraid of dyin'?" Hank asked.

"I guess he was, but he had a better chance with a parachute than he did ridin' a plane that was guaranteed to crash. I needed him to jump so I'd still have time to get out."

"Why didn't you leave him. . .just go ahead and jump?" Lonnie asked.

"I was the senior officer. I had to be the last one to leave the plane."

"What'd you do?" Lilli asked, spellbound.

"I pulled out my gun, aimed it at him, and said, 'You're goin' out of this plane one way or another. Now you better jump.'"

284

"Did he jump?"

"He did and I was right behind him."

"What happened next?"

"We got caught by the Swiss."

"Did they put you in prison?"

"It was an old hotel they had converted to an internment camp."

"That sounds pretty nice."

"It wasn't bad. You just couldn't leave. Men who tried to escape were sent to a real prison camp. We never saw them again, but we heard stories."

"So how'd you escape?" Walt asked.

"I paid one of the local boys to smuggle me in a Swiss Boy Scout uniform. Then I sneaked out and hiked up into the hills, pretending to be a Scout out explorin'. I climbed up into the mountains behind the town. When the mountains flattened out, I crawled across the fields for weeks until I made it into France."

"Bet you're as proud to be home as we are to have you," Flora commented.

"I'm goin' to buy a herd of cows and I'm never leavin' Arkansas again." John smiled, but no one doubted he was serious.

"What made you decide to escape?" Lilli asked.

John's eyes twinkled as he looked down at his bride. "Emily," he confessed.

"'Cause you missed her so much?" Clara sighed.

"'Cause she sent me a cablegram that said, "Hurry up. I'm getting tired of waitin'.""

When the laughter died down, Jake said, "Well, it's time to go to bed. Tomorrow's goin' to be a long day."

Chapter Thirty

October 1944

Flora's husband, Hugh, continued serving his time in the army as a medic. With her parents' agreement, Flora enrolled in beauty school to become a beautician. Every Sunday night she rode the bus seventeen miles to Blytheville. In exchange for her room and board there, she served meals to the other renters. Her day started with waiting breakfast. She had permission from the instructor to take an extended noon break, during which she hurried back to the house to get lunch on the table before going back to the school. When the class broke for supper, she again raced to the residence to help get food on the table. Her classes were in session until nine p.m. Upon her final return of an evening, she studied her chemistry books and memorized vocabulary until she could no longer keep her eyes open. Only then did she allow her exhausted body to rest. On Friday nights she took the bus back to Manila so she could work a half day as a shampoo girl in town. Flora wished her cousin's shop was open all of Saturday so she could earn a full day's pay.

"We're movin' again." Jake broke the news at breakfast. The announcement received a couple of sighs and one groan, but the children knew not to complain. It had been over fifteen years since the family had lost their land. These younger children had few if any memories of ever living in the same place for more than three or four years at a time.

Marina set a platter of fried eggs and another with bacon piled high on table. She motioned to Hank to pass the platter of buttermilk biscuits and bowl of milk gravy in front of him. She kept a straight face so as not to spoil Jake's surprise.

In a casual voice as if remarking that the hens had laid seventeen eggs, he mentioned, "This house has three bedrooms and an indoor bathroom." That got a reaction. The children erupted with questions. "Three bedrooms?" "Indoor bathroom? You mean it doesn't have an outhouse?" "Where is it?" "Does an inside bathroom work at night too?" "Can I have a bedroom to myself?" "When will we move?"

Marina laughed. Pleased with their excitement, Jake answered the questions. "Yes, three bedrooms *and* indoor plumbing, so no, you won't have to go outside to use an outhouse, not even at night. The house is located about two miles south of here and three-quarters of a mile east. It was built as the family's original home, but now they've built a bigger place and intend to use this as a sharecropping house. No one gets a room all to themselves—not even your mommy." He grinned at Marina.

For the next fifteen minutes excited voices planned what it would be like for eleven people to spread out among three bedrooms, kitchen, living room, and inside bathroom. They had seven children and two grandchildren living at home. This was going to be more space per person than they had since their family was small.

Marina listened to them chat for several minutes, then admonished, "Eat up now. You'll need your energy in the fields even if you are movin' to a fancy house." They gulped down their food, even the girls.

The wagon ride out to the fields felt like a parade. They were all exhilarated by the news. The children laughed and teased each other. Sammy beat the side of the wagon like a drum. Lilli and Clara shouted hello to every wagon they passed, including the migrant workers from the hills.

Once in the cotton patch, Sadie, as she often loved to do, burst into song at the top of her lungs. Marina never scolded her because singing didn't slow the girl down. In fact, the fun of listening to her sing made everyone's cotton picking go faster.

They hadn't enjoyed such a joyful transition for years. Their children always cooperated with what they were asked to do, but this time they were enthusiastic. Belongings were packed before it was necessary. Even Marina, who typically was far too busy to fool with celebrations, surprised the family with chocolate gravy the night before they moved.

The morning of the move, the landowner met them at the new house. "Welcome! Glad to have you here." Mr. Tate shook hands with Marina and Jake. His eyes drifted to the wagonload of children. As was often the case, you could almost see him counting. "My, my! Sally Ann was right. You sure do have a big bunch of children, don't you?"

"We have a fine bunch of children," Jake agreed.

"I see. Sure is a lot of 'em. Well, come on. Let me show you 'round the place."

Everyone exited the wagon. Curbing their excitement, they stepped onto the porch to begin the tour. Mr. Tate motioned with both arms. "Well, as you can see, this is the living room. Over there's the kitchen. Down here there's a bedroom on the left and a second one across the hall."

He started to move back toward the living room when Marina asked, "Is that the third bedroom at the end of the hall?"

"Well, yes," he hesitated. "There is a third room, but we've got it full of furniture and odds and ends the wife doesn't want to keep up at our new house. We piled all the extras in that back room so it'll be out of your way."

"Our agreement was for a three-bedroom house," Jake reminded him.

"It is a three-bedroom," Mr. Tate agreed, "but we need to keep our furniture in there right now. The missus says our older boy may want it when he gets married. You can make do with the two rooms. It's no different from what you're used to over at the Pliney farm." He hurried back to the front door.

"And the bathroom?" Jake asked.

"Got you a fine outhouse right out back."

"What about this bathroom inside?" Sadie spoke up, ignoring the look she was getting from her mother. "Isn't that a bathroom next to the third bedroom?"

"Oh, that doesn't work right—somethin' wrong with the plumbin'. I've got it locked up so you won't have to bother with it. You can use the two-seater out back. With such a big family, you'll like havin' space for two people to use at once." Marina's face burned, but again she said nothing. Jake's face had a cold look to it.

"Well, that's about it. Make yourselves at home. Jake, I'm lookin' forward to your getting' started with the plowin' on Monday morning. That's a good thing about you havin' so many children. Y'all take care." The screen door slammed.

"Well, let's get everythin; unpacked," Marina announced immediately. The welcome had left a bad taste in everybody's mouth and she wanted to wash it out with busyness. "Hank, Sammy, start bringin' in boxes. Girls, let's find a place for everythin'." The move that started out so happy now had a subdued tone. No one talked as they brought the boxes inside and unpacked. No one spoke about the rooms which were off limits.

During the next few days, Marina learned to ignore the bathroom and third bedroom. She simply pretended they didn't exist. Sadie, on the other hand, struggled. The girl's anger seemed to grow every time she walked down the hall. Marina heard her wondering, "Why don't they put their extra stuff in the barn? We're supposed to have the whole house. That's always been the sharecroppin' deal." Or Sadie would mutter, "I don't believe that bathroom is broken. I think they just don't want us to use it." Marina wanted to comfort her daughter, but she had no words that would be both honest and soothing, so she kept quiet.

Five days after they moved in, Sadie stood before her parents. "I knew it! I knew there was nothin' wrong with that bathroom. It works fine!"

"How do you know?" Marina questioned.

"I checked it," Sadie confessed. "I crawled through that back window and flushed the commode. Not a thing in the world wrong with it. It works fine. I think we ought to use it."

"You crawled through the window?" Marina gasped.

"Yes, ma'am. I wanted to prove there is nothin' wrong with that bathroom. It's fine, just a little dusty from being locked up. We can use that bathroom."

"No, ma'am, you will not use that bathroom," Jake corrected her. Mr. Tate said it's broken and whether it is or it isn't, that bathroom is off limits. You ever go in that bathroom again and I will tan your hide, girl. Is that clear?"

"But Pappy!" Sadie began to protest.

"But nothin'. I've spoken and that's the way it's going to be. Am I clear?"

"Yes, sir."

Marina understood Jake's not wanting them to use rooms where they were not welcome, but she also sympathized with Sadie and the other children. Sadie was right. It wasn't fair, but there was nothing they could do about it. They couldn't leave because they had nowhere else to go. All the other sharecropping cabins in the area were spoken for this season. Sadie looked miserably angry. Again, Marina wished there was something she could do to comfort her daughter, but she had nothing to offer. If only they hadn't been expecting this place to be different, there wouldn't have been any disappointment. "Come on, Sadie," Marina encouraged. "You can help me with the dishes."

. . .

Cotton production marched on. Government officials on the radio announced the Great Depression had ended with World War II, but not much of Marina's life had changed. The world and its seasons seem to revolve around how much money they made at the cotton gin. She still put out a big garden that fed her family. She still felt as though she was going ninety to nothing against the wind.

Jake was late getting home from the gin one night. Marina peered thru the window for what felt like the hundredth time. There must have been a lot of farmers ahead of him today. Maybe his being late was good news. It could mean the gin was giving a good price per pound and more farmers were going there to sell.

The children were in bed, so Marina picked up her scrap basket, settling down at the big hickory table. Lilli would need a new quilt to sleep under before winter, so she had best get started. She picked up Hank's old shirt and considered it for squares. It had a couple of stains but could yield half-a-dozen small patches. Marina picked up her scissors and began to cut. Lilli liked stars. She'd quilt in the Arkansas Star pattern. Next, Flora's first store-bought dress came out of the rag basket. Flora had outgrown it years ago. Marina had remade it for Emily and then for Sadie. Too bad she had to cut it up. Well, it would make a good memory in the blanket. She smiled. That had been a pair of chickens well worth selling.

Marina glanced at the clock. Eight o'clock. Perhaps someone from the county extension office was sharing a new idea about how to get a higher yield per acre. Or, he might have run into Emily's John. Those two always got on well. Nine-thirty. Jake should have been home long before now even if he stopped to chat with some of the men and time got away from him.

Marina picked up an old dress of Clara's. There wasn't enough to remake into a shirt and no one small enough to

294

remake it for. Those days had passed for her and Jake. Marina's thoughts turned to little Joey. Her eyes still burned with unshed tears when she thought of him. She brushed at her lashes and selected several other items to cut into blocks. If she didn't use these pieces for Lilli, they'd be ready for the wedding ring pattern. She suspected Roy would be announcing his plans soon.

After all the old clothes had been cut into blocks, Marina laid them out on the table. She pieced her pattern and began sewing. The quilt and the night grew longer.

Roy gave a loud snore and the sound startled her. Needing to move she stood up. She checked each child and grandchild and then went back to work. She forced herself to continue to work and not pace the floor. A little after two o'clock in the morning, the sound of tires crunched over the road. An automobile in the middle of the night could only mean bad news. She couldn't see the driver until the sedan pulled right up beside the house. The door opened, and Jake stepped out. She rushed to meet him. "Are you alright? Where have you been?"

"Doin' business," he replied with an air of cockiness.

Confused, she motioned toward the automobile. "Who does this belong to?"

"Me," he announced grandly.

"You! Where did you get the money to buy an automobile?"

"From the gin," he grinned even bigger.

"You spent our cotton money on an automobile?" she asked, unable to believe her ears.

"Sure did," he assured her. "Benny Biddix and I got to talkin'
at the gin. He knows a man over in Osceola that sells 'em. We
drove over in Benny's car. He got me a good deal and I drove
home." He was bragging now.

She turned away. A good deal! What kind of a deal would
they get on all the things they normally bought with the
cotton money?

"Do you like it?" he asked, totally oblivious to her frustration.

"I'm tired," she responded. "Let's talk about it in morning."
She knew full well there wouldn't be any more to discuss in
the morning than there was tonight. She wasn't sure if she was
angrier about his spending money on a car or madder that she
had been so scared when she didn't know where he was.

Morning brought whoops of admiration from the children.
Marina stayed busy in the kitchen while the rest of the family
oohed and aahed over the purchase. Jake promised to teach each
of the boys how to drive and to take everyone for long rides.

The girls glanced nervously toward the house where their
mother continued to work. They understood no reaction was
clearly a big reaction, but like their brothers, they couldn't hide
their admiration for the automobile sitting in front of the house.

Feeling completely isolated and torn up on the inside,
Marina busied herself grinding hog meat for sausage. Next she
mixed in the right portion of fat before heaping salt, ground
peppercorns, and brown sugar high. She sifted the spices twice

to create an even blend. Soon the sweet, rich odor of their sausage filled the air.

Marina knew some husbands wasted cotton money every time they went to the gin. Jake hadn't exactly wasted it. He spent it on something she didn't believe they needed. Clearly, he thought they did. Exasperated, she over-spiced her pork.

The morning hours dragged on. She stuffed the fatty mix into casings. It would have been nice if one or two of the girls had come in to help, but none of them thought of it and she surely wasn't going out there to ask. She wanted nothing to do with that mess.

Eventually, the loneliness got to her. It was surprising how distant you could feel from a person only fifty yards away. Marina sighed again, this time with less vengeance. Jake was a good husband. He loved her and the children. He worked his tail off every day of every year for them.

From the window she saw Jake look toward the house. She knew her lack of enthusiasm had put a damper on his pride in presenting his family with such an extravagant gift.

Marina tied off the last casing. Enough! She and Jake had never allowed differences to create a rift between them. No good could come from doing it now. She took off her apron and hung it on a hook. Looking out the window, she caught him glancing toward the kitchen again.

She opened the screen door. Jake's eyes were on Marina as she strode toward him. He wasn't sure what she intended.

He didn't speak, but his eyes pleaded with her to understand. Nearby, Lilli and Clara begged for a second ride. "Please, Pappy," they coaxed, "take us for another drive."

Marina gave her husband a warm smile as she answered the question for him. "After me, girls."

At breakfast a few days later, she made her announcement. "We are going to buy a piano." Everyone looked at her in amazement. Lilli clapped her hands. Marina continued. "Lilli needs a piano to practice on even when school is not in session." She stood up, walked over to the counter and picked up an empty coffee can. "This is for our piano money. I'm sure all of you will want to contribute each time you get paid for pickin' cotton or any other work you get the chance to do." Her tone was pleasant but left no doubt that she expected regular contributions from every one of her children. "The piano won't be a new one, but it will play."

"Are you going to pay for it on time?" Clara asked.

"No!" Marina responded sharply. "We'll pay cash." Her voice softened, "It won't take long with everybody helpin'. Lilli, you can keep track of how much money is in the can."

Contributing to the "Piano Can" turned out to be a great competition among the brothers and sisters. As expected, everyone donated part of their regular earnings, but they also found other ways to fill the can faster. Flora put in half of her Saturday tips from the beauty salon. The younger ones did chores for the neighbors. Marina put in both her egg and butter money. Rosa Lee even sent a whole dollar in the mail. With all this focused saving, they met their goal in a little over a year.

The whole family cheered when the piano arrived from Paragould. Marina was as excited as Lilli. She was thrilled when the girl sat down on the bench. Since Lilli practiced and took her lessons at school, Marina had never heard her play. She spent the day dusting the house just to be near the music. To her ears, not even Chopin could have sounded more beautiful.

. . .

More winters melted into more springs. One morning, the sound of giggling voices, rustling paper, and hushed secrets made Marina turn from the stove to see what the ruckus was all about. Emily, Sadie, Lilli, and Clara were holding a box wrapped with a bow. "Surprise!"

"What's this?" Their joy infected Marina.

"It's for you, Mommy," they chorused. "It's an early Mother's Day present."

"You'll never guess," Lilli teased.

Her daughters paraded her to a chair, demanding she open her present. Marina carefully slipped a cheery ribbon off the side of the box without breaking it. "I can't imagine," she murmured. She lifted the lid. Under layers of tissue whiter than cotton, lay a silky dress the color of cranberries.

Marina drew in her breath. It was so soft, so beautiful. Everyone began talking at the same time. "It's from all of us!" "Try it on!" "Yes, try it on!"

They pushed her laughing and protesting to the bedroom where they helped her change clothes. The silk felt light, airy, almost as if there was nothing to it.

"What do you think?" "Do you like the feel of silk?" "Do the sleeves fit well?" The girls continued talking over each other.

"It's beautiful!" Marina whispered.

They were so absorbed in the success of their surprise that no one heard Jake walk in until he spoke, his tone stern and cold. "Where did you get that dress?"

"The girls surprised me. Isn't it lovely?"

"Take it back!"

"What?" Marina was as shocked at his reaction as the girls.

"No wife of mine is going to wear a scarlet dress like some dance hall girl!" He stormed out the door, charging toward the barn before they could react.

Marina stood frozen for a moment after the screen door slammed. Then, she slipped the dress off. Gently folding the delicate material, she replaced the tissue and closed the box. She pulled her house dress back on and announced, "Thank you, girls, for thinkin' of me. I'd better get dinner started."

"Why is he so mad?" "We bought it 'specially for you." "You looked so beautiful in it." "This isn't fair!"

"That's enough, girls!" Marina's frustration came out in harsh tones echoing her husband. She felt angry with him for hurting the girls. Jake's reaction hadn't made any more sense to her than it had to them, but she would never allow them to criticize their father. "Your father has spoken."

For the first time in the history of their marriage, he lay with his back to her. The sound of uneven breathing revealed that he too was unable to sleep. Marina stared up at the ceiling, aching for things to be normal between them again. She grieved over this rift in their relationship. She hurt but her heart also cried for his pain.

Sighing deeply, she decided to break the silence before it broke her. "Jake, the girls didn't intend to make you angry. They wanted to surprise me with a store-bought dress. They didn't mean anything by the color. I doubt if they even know there's any significance to a red dress other than it's bright and cheerful like a pansy."

Jake turned towards her. His words were gruff, but his tone begged her to understand. "Marina, my mother wore red when she'd go out. She'd leave all of us kids at home, even the little ones, to go out and dance. All she thought about was herself and havin' a good time. She was a bad mother. I knew when she put on that red dress that she'd be leavin' us to go down the street to dance.

301

"I worry about our girls, Marina. I worry they'll have something of my mother in them. I want them all to be like you—kind, loving mothers who take care of their children."

"You don't have to worry about our daughters, Jake. They're fine, upstandin' girls. They've never given us any trouble. Their children will be proud of them just as we're proud of them now."

"But what if they do have somethin' of my mother in them?" he cried out, his secret fear surfacing.

Marina reached out to touch her husband's face. "If our children have somethin' of your mother in them, then it will be the curl of their hair or the color of her eyes. Our girls know right from wrong, Jake. We've taught them good values. You can trust that our daughters will always be good women."

Slipping his arm around her shoulders, Jake pulled her close so her head rested on his chest. "I know they are." He sighed. "Marina, I saw you in that red dress and it was like the past just swallowed me up."

"I don't need to wear red dresses if they stir up bad memories for you."

"Our daughters are sweet, beautiful, smart young women. They will all be good mothers just like you."

"They're also smart like their pappy," Marina whispered.

"Smartest thing I ever did was marry you," Jake admitted.

Chapter Thirty-One

July 1946

The letter began:

Dear Dad,

I am living in Manila, Arkansas. My wife, Marina, and I have eleven children. If you're willing, I would like to see you again.

Your son, Jake

Three weeks later he received a reply:

Dear Jake,

I was glad to get your letter and know you are doing well. We all wondered what happened to you. I am sorry to have to tell you that your dad died during a freezing winter storm two years ago. We buried him out by his cabin. Your sisters and brother are doing well. They all have families now. Alice and Florence live here in the county. Their husbands have good jobs. Evelyn moved out to California, where she's a hairdresser. Your brother, Jesse, is still riding the rails looking for adventure. He drops in every once in a while. I'll let the girls know where you are living. I'm sure they would like to hear from you. I'm sorry I can't tell you anything about your mother. I haven't kept up with her since your mom and dad divorced. I expect your sisters can tell you something if you are interested. If you are ever back up in Indiana, please come see me. Take care.

Your Uncle Bill.

Jake bowed his head. "I waited two years too late."

Five days after that another letter arrived:

Our Dear Brother,

Thank heaven we have finally found you. I will never forget that day Mother threw you out of the house. I was only eight and you were twelve. You seemed so big and grownup to me. Now I realize you weren't more than a kid yourself. I stood at the window watching as you walked down the street away from us. Since that moment I have been afraid I would never see my big brother again. Florence, Jesse, and I have missed you. Evelyn doesn't remember much since she was just a toddler when you left, but we told her stories about you—how you would do chores for neighbors and buy us a Tootsie Roll from the Mercantile. One time you even bought a Hershey's chocolate bar that we split amongst ourselves. Jesse loves to talk about how you and he climbed the hills and explored the caves when we lived in Mitchell. Of course, you always watched out for us, especially when Mother went dancing. We are so glad you didn't forget us. Now that we know where you are, Florence and I would like to come for a visit. Would that be alright with your wife? When can we come?

I remain your devoted sister,
Alice

Marina scoured the house from top to bottom. She destroyed every weed that even thought about growing near her flowers. Even the henhouse received fresh hay. She wanted the sisters to see for themselves what a fine man Jake turned out to be.

As the day drew nearer, Jake became quieter and more introspective. Marina left him alone, knowing he had a lot of memories to sift through.

More Hartmanns than just Clara were peeking out a window when the 1946 forest green Oldsmobile turned onto their gravel drive. Even before her husband turned the engine off, a lady with soft brown curls brushed back from her face jumped out of the front passenger seat. She wore a close-fitted hat with a fabric rose on the front, coordinated with a green-and-white-print dress. Her anxious eyes searched for the big brother she had almost given up for lost.

More slowly, the door to the backseat opened, and a tall woman wearing a fitted jacket with padded shoulders and matching skirt stepped out. She appeared tentative, unsure they were really welcome. Not wanting to intrude on a private reunion, the brother-in-law took his time exiting from the driver's seat of the Oldsmobile.

Marina watched the scene unfolding before her. She felt Jake's presence beside her. He seemed hesitant, almost afraid to move forward. She knew her husband well enough to know he was wondering if perhaps too many years had passed for a reunion of sibling hearts. Without a word, she put her hand on his back, rubbing it gently. That was all the encouragement he needed. Jake shot out the screen door and across the porch to the little sisters he had left behind.

Eventually, Jake and his sisters entered the house, with the brother-in-law trailing. Introductions were made and the reunited family took their seats in the living room. Marina, along with her older girls, busied themselves in the kitchen pouring fresh-ground coffee and cutting generous pieces of cherry pie topped with fresh cream. The aroma of dinner filled the house, promising a feast to come.

Jake sat on the end of the sofa with Alice and her husband to his right. Florence settled on the rocker, but inched it closer to the couch, leaning forward so she wouldn't miss a word. As it was, she and Alice did most of the talking, catching Jake up on their lives, filling him in on the brother and sister who weren't able to make the trip with them.

At one point, the girls talked about their mother. Nellie Hartmann had married several times since her divorce. Once, she had been widowed. The other marriages had ended in divorce. Currently, she was on husband number six. The sisters were not sure exactly where she was living, but they knew from experience she would turn up when the marriage no longer pleased her and she was in need of money. Marina quietly signaled her girls they were all needed in the kitchen. They didn't need to hear old family scandals.

306

Much to Marina's relief, and probably Jake's too, Alice moved the conversation on to a retelling of childhood shenanigans. The sisters reminded him about playing Cowboys and Indians and King of the Mountain. Jake sat quietly, listening intently, soaking up the joy of reclaiming his status as big brother. Glancing in from the kitchen, Marina thought she could almost see his heart being healed.

Dinner turned out to be every bit the feast Marina had envisioned. She robbed her storehouse, roasting a beef AND baking a ham. For side dishes she served fried potatoes, sweet corn, green beans and bacon, sugar-glazed carrots, mashed potatoes with gravy, deep-fried pigs feet, fried zucchini, fresh tomatoes, a quart of her homemade applesauce, salad, pickles (dill and sweet), and hogshead cheese. If she had it in her garden or her cellar, a plate of it appeared on the table. Marina was grateful Jake's family had come at the end of summer when the garden's harvest was at its height. For dessert she served lemon meringue pie along with chocolate cake topped with roasted nuts the children had gathered for her. Marina was satisfied she had everything a guest could want.

The visit went well. Alice admired the girls' cotton dresses and Marina's patchwork quilts. Florence looked a bit anxious when she had to walk out back to use the outhouse. She came back quickly and had a whispered conversation with Alice, who dug into her purse and produced some tissue paper before Florence walked back outside. Marina called Clara over to her. "You made sure there were plenty of pages in the Sears & Roebuck catalogue, didn't you?"

Their guests left just before twilight. Marina thought it was sad that they missed sitting on the porch during the best part of the day, but they had wanted to start back north before dark. Marina fell into bed exhausted, but satisfied.

A month later, Marina was shucking corn when a letter arrived along with a corrugated cardboard box from Indiana. "How nice," she murmured. "They sent a thank you note and looks like a gift for Jake. Perhaps it's something that belonged to his father." Smiling, she opened the envelope. Just as she suspected, the sisters thanked them all for a lovely visit. Marina lit up with satisfaction at the success. The letter gave updates on what everyone in the family was doing and again emphasized how grateful they were to be reunited with Jake and to meet his family. A post script addressed to Marina read, "We are sending all the clothes and blankets we could spare and trust this will help you with the children during the winter. We are sorry we couldn't send more. Perhaps in the future as our children outgrow their clothes."

Aghast, Marina sat down in the chair. She was mortified. They didn't believe she and Jake could take care of their children! Why on earth did they think that? Marina reviewed every detail of the visit in her mind. The children had all looked beautiful in neatly pressed Sunday clothes. Not one of them had a hair out of place. No one had even the tiniest rip or stain. She'd personally checked them herself. No, the children were fine. There was nothing to criticize there. Surely dinner was sufficient. She couldn't think of anything else that could have been added to her table. Had two meats not been enough? Should she have baked a chicken? She'd thought about it, but three meats seemed like braggin' and she hadn't known what the sisters' financial situations were. She hadn't wanted to embarrass them.

Feeling disgraced, Marina stood up and pushed the brown box into a corner of the kitchen without even going through it. She couldn't throw it out because it was a gift from Jake's sisters, but she sure didn't have to dig through it like a dog and rub her nose in the humiliation.

Her children, on the other hand, were thrilled with the surprise. They begged to examine the contents. "No, you may not," she told them. "Just let it be." Jake can deal with this himself when he comes in from the field, she thought with satisfaction.

But Jake didn't deal with it when he came home. "That was nice of them," he commented while Marina's face quietly burned with shame.

Marina never left anything out of place in her house. The sharecroppers' cabins she had lived in had all been small, but they were also neat and spot clean. Every item in the house had its place, and it returned there the second it was no longer in use. When any of her acquaintances complained they didn't have enough space to keep things clean, she always thought to herself that if you couldn't keep a small house clean, you wouldn't be able to keep a big one clean either. But this box was different. It sat there in the corner of the kitchen. It sat for days. It sat there and annoyed her every time she walked past it.

One afternoon while Marina canned the last of the season's green beans, Sadie slipped into the kitchen and sat down by the box. Marina could see her out of the corner of her eye but ignored her. Like a cat sneaking up on its prey, Sadie eased her hand into the box and pulled out the first thing it touched. It was a green wool skirt, pretty, but too small even for Clara. Sadie refolded the item, setting it aside before pulling out the next. This time it was a sparkly hair bow that couldn't possibly go with clothes the girls owned. That was a quick toss into the "no" pile. Next, Sadie pulled out a stained handkerchief that wouldn't even make a good quilt square. It was tossed straight into the trash. Well, at least she's being discerning, Marina thought. The investigation continued — a ruffled white blouse that might fit Lilli, a worn blanket, an apron. A pair of fashionable high-heeled shoes that wouldn't survive a walk to church was pushed aside.

Then Sadie reached in and pulled out a pair of women's navy blue dress pants. Pants! Sadie had never owned a pair in her life. The girl scrambled to her feet pulling the slacks on. She stretched and admired them. She walked back and forth beside the table. Marina begrudgingly admitted to herself that the pants fit her well, but she still pretended to ignore the fashion show. The last items to appear out of the box were another blanket, a little girl's coat, and two more shirts for boys.

Sadie kept the slacks on after making quick work of the box's contents. She distributed the clothes that fit her sisters, tucked the ones that wouldn't fit anybody into the rags basket, and hauled the cardboard box out to the barn where it could eventually be used to store something. Marina stewed about it for a few minutes and then decided, well, at least she wouldn't have to look at the blasted thing anymore.

. . .

With money saved from her two jobs as a hairdresser, Flora put a down payment on a two-bedroom house in town on Olympia Street. She, Virginia, and Lonnie moved in a few days later. Marina knew Flora wanted a home for her family ready when her husband returned from the war. But Marina, instead of luxuriating in the space with three fewer people to house, felt the emptiness of missing them.

Flora and her children stopped by late one afternoon for a visit. "Mommy, I was thinking about going to the revival over at the Baptist Church tonight. Would you and Pappy like to go with me?"

She must not want to go alone, a married woman with no husband along, Marina thought. "I believe we could do that," Marina agreed.

Virginia and Lonnie opted to stay home with their aunts, so it was just the three who filed into the wooden pew. "Our scripture for tonight is from Psalm 139:23-24," the evangelist announced. "'Search me, O God, and know my heart: try me, and know my thoughts: And see if there be any wicked way in me, and lead me in the way everlasting.'" The sermon was a good one although perhaps not the most scholarly one any of them had ever heard. The congregation stood for the invitation and the pianist softly began to play "Just As I Am."

Marina felt a soft tugging at her heart, a desire for something more. She and Jake had lived good moral lives. They had no heinous crimes to confess, no startling confessions to make. Even so, in that moment, Marina understood their goodness had not been enough to secure a relationship with God. She wanted more. Compelled to the cross, Marina wanted Jesus. Sure as the ocean she had never seen, Marina felt the power of the living God wash over her, wiping out the sin, fears, disappointments, and even the inadequacies of a lifetime.

She looked up at Jake. He nodded and they stepped out into the aisle with Flora a footfall behind them.

Chapter Thirty-Two

October 1950

T he years tumbled over each other. Clara was the last child to marry, and Marina, who had been raising children for forty years, found herself at somewhat of a loss to be without them. How strange it seemed to cook for only two, to complete tasks without interruption, and to linger over meals to the conversation's end. That said, she was surprised at how easily she adapted to a life with just her and Jake. It reminded her of the close companionship they had experienced during the early years of their marriage.

Rural America changed after World War II. Farming corporations plowed over family farms, cultivating acreage that could cover a city. Advances in technology replaced hand labor with machines, squeezing sharecroppers off the land. Families like the Hartmanns could almost have done without their portion of cash from the cotton crop. Most of the money was used to pay off the spring seed anyway. But they could not do without a cabin or the space to plant a family garden.

The grown Hartmann children spread out in search of other hard work. Rosa Lee's family settled in Michigan, where her husband worked in a factory that made bowling pins. Flora and her husband rented out their house in Manila and moved to Indiana close to where Walt was living. The men found work in steel mills. Sadie and her husband tried farming for a few years but gave it up in favor of St. Louis factory jobs that guaranteed a consistent paycheck. Roy's family lived in West Memphis, Arkansas. Hank, Sammy, and Clara also tried life up north, but the South called them home. Lilli and Emily never left Mississippi County.

This new generation of local farmers prided themselves on being up-to-date on the latest technology. They made it their goal to modernize their holdings. The landowner the Hartmanns were working for bought a tractor and Jake learned to drive it.

Marina and Jake had been too busy to notice, but they were getting older. Marina frowned at the brown spots appearing on her hands and the wrinkles deepening her face. She noticed Jake moving a little slower. Cataracts had begun to cloud his vision.

"I feel like age sneaked up on us," Jake commented. "Where were we when that happened?"

Marina laughed. "In the cotton field, I expect."

. . .

Late one afternoon Marina was scrubbing sweet potatoes for dinner when she heard Jake come in. "You're home early," she teased. Turning around to face him she noticed his skin looked gray. He slumped wearily into a chair. She was beside him in a moment. "What's the matter?"

"I had an accident with the tractor," he confessed.

"Are you alright?"

He nodded, obviously still shook up. "I was down on the south end of town, tryin' to swing that turn from Route 18 onto Baltimore Street. Marina, I couldn't see it. Everythin' was too hazy. I didn't see the other car."

Marina ached for him. She could see he felt such a heaviness of heart. "Was anyone hurt?"

"No, but when I took the tractor back to the barn, Mr. Farnsworth said they won't be needin' me any longer. Marina, I've been let go. I don't have a job farmin' anymore. That's the only thing I know how to do. When the other landowners hear about this accident, I won't be able to get another place."

Unsure what to say, Marina patted his shoulder. Jake continued, "He said we can stay in the cabin until the end of the week."

She glanced around the room. The cabin itself was no great loss. They'd lived in nicer and they'd lived in worse, but they did need to live somewhere. She patted his shoulder again and went to pour him a strong cup of black coffee.

The children would to have to know. She winced at the thought of how much Jake would hate that. He was a humble man, but this was understandably a burning blow to his pride. Well, she could do it for him and spare him the telling.

But Marina never could have predicted this grief would turn into such a blessing. She told the children, and Emily's John promptly mentioned he needed a good man on his farm. He offered Jake a job and put him back on the tractor. Flora called long-distance from Indiana. The renters had moved out of her house in Manila and she would appreciate it so much if her parents would move in and keep up the property for her.

Their new home was a sweet, gray clapboard bungalow near downtown. A good-sized wash house stood twenty feet from the back of the dwelling. Jake enclosed the chicken coop with a wire fence. It wouldn't do to have their hens wandering off downtown. The property included a large garage Flora's husband had used to repair cars and plenty of land, so they didn't have to skimp on the size of their garden. Marina planted flowers around the house and bordered both sides of the sidewalk to the street.

They were surprised to discover how much they enjoyed the conveniences of living in town. One afternoon Marina ran into two old friends at the grocery. Marina, Norita McElvain, and her sister Lucille Culpepper had all gone to school together.

The women chatted for a minute before being interrupted by Norita's grandson tugging on her sleeve. "Meemaw, can we buy some of these and eat corn on the cob for dinner tonight?"

Norita looked down at the ear of corn he was holding up. "Child, don't you know the difference between field corn and eatin' corn?" She shook her head and looked at the other women. "Have you ever seen such a thing? I don't know what those children are learnin' in school. They spend twice as much time there and learn half as much as we did."

"I know what you mean." Lucille's head bobbed vigorously. "The other day, my granddaughter Barbara, she's visitin' from Memphis, asked why there were only a dozen eggs in the hen house. I said, 'Why honey, I only have fourteen hens. A dozen eggs is a pretty good day's work.' She said, 'Grandma, don't each hen lay a dozen eggs a day?' I thought, law, have mercy. Can you imagine a child fifteen years old who don't know a hen lays one egg a day when it decides to lay!"

"And a hen who lays two eggs in a day causes you to take notice," Norita declared. The ladies all nodded in agreement.

"Old Man Grueler claimed he had a chicken that laid an egg ever' day for sixty-four days straight, but I don't believe it." Lucille continued, "He was always telling stories."

"Not half of 'em true," her sister added as though she had personally done the math on his tales.

Marina was still smiling over the conversation as she walked home. She looked down toward her house and saw her brother

Wade's car in the drive. Pleased and immediately planning what she could pull out for supper, she hastened her steps.

Her guests were inside on the sofa conversing with Jake. "Good to see you," Marina greeted them. "You'll stay for supper, won't you?"

"No, afraid we can't today. We need to get back out to the farm," Wade answered.

"Where's Mama?" Marina asked, looking around. "Didn't she come to town with you?"

"That's what I wanted to talk to you about." Wade took a deep breath, before speaking fast. "Marina, we decided to put Mama in the Manila Nursing Home."

"Put Mama in a nursing home?" Marina was shocked at her brother's words. "What do you mean?"

"Well, she's gettin' older now. She needs to be somewhere safe—some place with a nurse nearby if she needs help."

"Bring Mama here. I'll take care of her."

"No, we've already decided."

"Who decided?" Marina's head was whirling.

"Twyla Fay and I did. Marina, you need to realize we've been takin' care of Mama ever since I married. It's too hard on Twyla Fay now. What about when Mama gets where she can't do for herself? She's a big woman. Twyla Fay won't be able to lift her or move her. We can't watch her all the time. She'll be better off. She wouldn't have broken her arm if she'd been in a nursing home."

"Mama broke her arm because that old cow kicked her while she was milkin' it."

"Yes, and I told Mama not to milk that cow, but she did it anyway."

Marina held her temper and tried not to sound accusatory. "You were in the fields late that day. A cow that's not been milked on time is miserable."

"That's beside the point."

"What will Mama say when you tell her?" Marina asked.

"She just said, 'Alright.' You know Mama's never been one to make much of a fuss."

"You already told her even before you talked to me about it?"

Twyla Fay broke in to the conversation. "Well, I am the one she's been livin' with for almost thirty-five years," she commented in a tight voice.

"Yes, I remember when you married and moved into the farmhouse with her," Marina's voice was every bit as icy as her sister-in-law's. "Fortunately, Mama had the farm for the two of you to move into."

"Now we did that to take care of her," Wade's tone held a slight reprimand. "And we've been takin' good care of her ever since."

"And Mama's been takin' care of you as well. She's the one who planted your garden and canned every vegetable in it." Marina turned back to her sister-in-law in an attempt to appeal to her womanly gratitude. "Twyla Fay, Mama watched over every one of your babies so you could be out in the fields with your husband."

"Marina," Wade interrupted, his voice stern now. "Mama's okay. She likes her room at the nursing home. She knows a lot of people there. It's much better than bein' stuck out on a farm with us. Here in town she's even closer to you. You can visit her any time you want."

"Are you sayin' you already moved her into that nursing home?" Marina felt anger sweep over and threaten to drown her. "Jake and I would have taken her."

"Now Marina, you are not big enough to pick Mama up if she fell on the floor. It's better this way."

Marina could not believe the rage she felt toward her own brother. She wished they would leave. She wanted to rush over to the nursing home to see her mother.

Twyla Fay nodded to Wade. "I think we best be goin'."

Jake walked them to the door. Marina sat on the sofa shaking from anger, then abruptly jumped up and crossed the few steps to the kitchen. She cut thick slices of ham from yesterday's dinner and slid them between buttermilk biscuits. Next, she heated a serving of black-eyed peas, spooning it into a bowl. She placed these items in a basket, adding a slice of apple pie. "I'm goin' to see Mama," she announced and let the screen door bang behind her. Jake would understand the slam wasn't directed toward him.

Marina coped with the anguish over her mother being in a nursing home by doing acts of service. Each day, regardless of the weather, she walked to the facility. She took Hattie offerings of homemade food on each visit. Sometimes it was a slice of cake or pie. Other times she took a jar of something she had preserved or a tomato picked fresh from her garden.

As much as she loved the joy of Hattie living so close, Marina still agonized over her mother's residence in a nursing home. Moving from a farm with chores that had to be done continually to a small room where she sat in a chair all day caused Hattie's health to decline quickly. Perhaps her constitution had already been deteriorating and Marina hadn't noticed because Hattie was so active. Certainly she had noticed her mother's failing eyesight. Unfortunately, it wasn't long before Wade's words were accurate. Marina could not have adequately met her mother's physical needs.

But during their visits, they still enjoyed time together. Mother and daughter had long talks remembering life at Big Lake, Marina's childhood on the farm near town, and years spent sharecropping; but mostly Hattie wanted to know about the present. She wanted to hear what the youngest children of the family were learning in school. New inventions especially interested her, and she shook her head in wonder when President Kennedy announced America's plan to put a man on the moon and return him safely to earth before the end of the decade.

.   .   .

These were kind years filled with gentle days. Jake built rows of shelves in the wash house to give Marina space for empty canning jars and room to store her many preserves. They spent most of their time tending the garden, making small repairs on the house, and taking care of each other.

Marina and Jake were still interested in, but no longer worried about, the fluctuating price of cotton. They were shocked when Arkansas changed the school year to a single session, September through June, instead of the split sessions which had accommodated the cotton plantings and harvests. Marina and Jake wondered how families could possibly manage.

Naturally, they kept up with family. They loved hearing about Flora's youngest daughter, June, twirling her baton for the high school squad. They were amazed at the detailed model airplanes Emily's eldest son built. They held their breath when Sadie revealed her three little girls could water ski! Not wanting to be intrusive, Jake and Marina rarely asked questions, but they enjoyed knowing what the children, the grandchildren, and the great-grandchildren were all up to.

Most of all, Marina and Jake enjoyed the time together. Life had not turned out the way they had planned. Their marriage had been born with the innocent belief that love would command life to go well. Then adversity arrived and scoured the naiveté out of them. But as the years passed, perseverance polished their union richly. Half a century of loving blended their lives in a way nothing but time can do.

December 1963

Finished with breakfast, Jake scooted back his chair. "Old-timers disease is gettin' to me," he told Marina. "I'm more tired this mornin' than I was when we went to bed last night." He stretched. "My arms and chest feel kinda tight." He took a deep breath. "I'll go get started plantin' the last of those spring bulbs out front. Maybe that'll work the kinks out of me."

Marina nodded and smiled. "I'll finish up here in the kitchen and be out to help you directly." She placed the clean black iron skillet back on the stove and turned the gas flame underneath it on low. This skillet had served her a good many years, and there was no reason to let any moisture cause it to rust.

Jake creaked to his feet with a grin and shuffled out the screen door. She watched him out the kitchen window as he made his way to the garage. He reappeared with his tools as she put dishes in the cupboard. Focused on his purpose, he moved across the yard a little faster.

Marina had the kitchen put to rights within ten minutes. With a few deft movements she wrung out her dishrag, hanging it neatly over the center of the double sink. With the inside done, she refocused, imagining how the front of their house would look in March. She always treasured that moment when the first crocus peeked above the still-brown ground. Perhaps a bunch of daffodils on either side of the porch would brighten the front a little more. She'd mention it to Jake.

Marina opened the front door and started down the steps before she saw him. Halfway down the sidewalk Jake lay crumpled on the ground. He was gone.

Chapter Thirty-Three

December 1963

Marina went through the motions, going where she was led, thanking people for their kindness. "She's handlin' it well," someone whispered in a voice not intended for her, but with a volume impossible for her to have missed. *Handling it well?* Marina wondered. What did that mean? How could one *handle* death at all?

She wanted the casket in the living room where she could sit up with Jake all night, but Walt overruled her, making arrangements with a funeral home. "You'll sleep better," he predicted. But she didn't.

The service was lost in a blur. People talked about what a good man he had been, such a loving husband and devoted father. Everything they said was true, but it was almost as though they were talking about a stranger. They spoke in past tense. "He *was* a good neighbor." He *helped* everyone he could.

This couldn't be her Jake they were talking about. Jake could never be past tense. He was too much of her. If he was totally gone, then she would be too. Her body stayed in the chair, but emotionally she detached.

Marina's mind wandered back over the last few years at the cottage on Olympia. It was owned by Flora, but everyone thought of it as "Granny and Grandpa Hartmann's house." No landowner could decide when their work there was complete. They had settled in as though the house was a member of the family. She and Jake belonged there.

Fear crept in, bringing her back to the present. If she had to move again, it would feel like losing a part of Jake. As soon as the service was over, she sought out her daughter. "Flora, I don't want to break up housekeeping. I want to stay in the house," she pleaded.

"Mommy, you can stay right there as long as you want. You don't ever have to move if you don't want to," Flora assured her.

The casket was lowered into the ground. After most of the people turned away, Marina stood beside the grave, feeling the finality of the ceremony. She already felt a sense of loss, but now a panic rushed over her. What if she lost Jake's grave the way she had lost little Joey's? What if she came back in a month and couldn't find the place where they'd laid him? She stood there memorizing the landscape. Walt gently tugged at her sleeve, but she resisted. She had to know she could find the grave again. This time she ignored the trees, focusing on buildings

326

that had been constructed since they buried little Joey. When she was satisfied, and not a moment before, she allowed them to lead her away.

Most of the children stayed a day or two after the funeral. Finally, they were all gone, every beloved child, every precious grandchild, every well-meaning in-law. She was alone, an aloneness deeper than any she had ever experienced before. With the children all back with their own families and responsibilities, there was no one left to anticipate and provide for her every need. The sun came up, requiring her bed to be made. The hens laid eggs that needed to be cooked. The garden had to be prepared for planting. Regardless of the pain, life did not allow one to stop.

Marina went about her tasks numbly at first, silently resisting life's pull back into active participation. When Clara had another baby, Marina wondered what about this child would echo Jake. For a moment, she forgot he was lying in the cemetery and spoke to him. Then she remembered and felt foolish and lonelier than ever. But those moments when she sensed his presence happened again and again. The veil between them hung thin. His presence felt real and called her out of heart-wrenching grief. Marina slipped into the comforting knowledge that Jake was so much a part of her that he could never be completely away. This separation was temporary. Inscribed on his tombstone was the promise, "We will meet again."

Five months after the funeral, Flora returned to Arkansas, determined to make changes for her mother's comfort. She brought Virgina and her daughter's two little ones with her.

Flora hired contractors to improve the house. She was adding a full bath and a dining room and expanding one of the bedrooms. "Poor Pappy!" she lamented. "He lived his whole life and never had indoor plumbing. I should have put a bathroom in sooner. I kept thinkin' I'd get to the improvements next year."

"It's all right," Marina tried to console her.

Without answering, Flora shook her head and began to sweep construction dust into a pile.

Marina stepped out into the side yard, careful to stay out of the way of men putting new siding on the house. How do you answer those feelings of guilt? How do you tell your child that this remarkable gift of convenience she has just given you isn't a distinguishing factor in your life? She and Jake had lived in so many houses during their life together—in the woods, over near Floodway, near Buffalo Ditch. They had even lived in three different green houses all on the same road and a couple of cabins twice. They always thought they were a step closer to a home of their own until the greed of her cousin washed that dream away with more finality than a Mississippi flood.

Somewhere in the years after they lost the house, sometime after she had accepted the certainty that Jake would never agree to purchase another homestead, came the realization that they were each other's home. And then, only after the dream of ownership was gone, had they received this gift of a permanent house. Fulfillment came with the letting go.

It really was okay that Jake had never lived with an indoor commode. How do you ease the guilt of an adult child embroiled in the daily rush and pressure of completing tasks? Marina shook her head. Perhaps you are not supposed to teach them. Maybe the young need those dreams so they can learn it is possible to survive without fulfilling some of them. Perhaps only very old women understand there is also value in the dreams that are not fulfilled.

"Granny," Flora's three-year-old granddaughter called from the edge of the garden where she was patting dirt together with a spoon. "Was this you and Grandpa Hartmann's dream home?"

Marina laughed. "Yes, honey. I guess it was." Well, she amended her thoughts, perhaps this wisdom is understood by very old women *and* very young ones too.

A year and a half after losing Jake, death struck again. Hattie was ninety-two years old when she was laid to rest in the Manila Cemetery. Marina herself was sixty-nine years of age. Still, Marina grieved deeply. No one is ever ready to lose a mother. Marina found herself asking the question death always brings: How can this be the end? Instinctively, we know it cannot.

The number of family members expanded yearly or, truth be told, often monthly. Walt bragged that the total of Jake and Marina Hartmann's descendants might soon reach one hundred.

August 1973

As spread out as they were, Marina's children all made it a point to get home every year. Flora came for two weeks in August, bringing her thirteen-year old granddaughter Katie.

"I'd like to take some Arkansas catfish back to Indiana with us," Flora commented. So the day before they left, Flora, Marina, and Katie drove over to Lake City. They picked their way down the worn path to the St. Francis where a fishing shack built of planks snuggled close to the bank.

A river man appeared in the open doorway. He was about sixty years old with a somewhat-trimmed gray beard. His sharp eyes appraised them for sales potential. He nodded respectfully to the women. "Ladies," he asked, "What can I do for you this afternoon?"

"Do you have thirty pounds of fresh catfish?" Flora asked.

"Yes, ma'am, right here." He gestured to a large plastic tub filled with river water. The women peered in to see catfish swimming in circles.

"Do you do all your own fishin'?" Flora inquired.

"Yes, ma'am."

Flora nodded. "When did you catch these?"

"Caught ever' one of 'em this mornin'." He pointed a stubby finger toward the middle of the river. "Right around that bend over there."

"Alright then. I'll take thirty pounds."

"Yes, ma'am. You tell me which fish you want and I'll pull 'em out for you."

"That big one there looks good," Flora pointed. "And those two." She indicated a couple more.

Katie's attention began to wander as her grandmother carefully selected the fish she would cart home to Indiana. Suddenly her eyes lit on a houseboat painted bright blue and trimmed in ornate red gingerbread. "Oh," she exclaimed. "That's beautiful!"

The old river man looked over at the boat of ill repute. Unsure how to respond, he gave the girl a non-committal grunt.

Katie continued. "That is the most beautiful boat I have ever seen in my life." She looked at the river man, "Have you ever seen it before?"

Uneasy, the man nodded.

"That is gorgeous." The girl would not stop. "When I grow up I want to live on that boat," she announced.

"No, you don't!" The river man knew the answer to that.

"Oh, yes, I do," Katie insisted. "I just love it!" She was quiet for a moment, then asked the man, "Have you ever been inside that boat before?"

The man sputtered a non-response at the same time that Flora, who had been trying to ignore the conversation, burst out, "Katherine, hush!"

To the relief of all grown-ups, Katherine finally hushed.

Marina looked down at the ground. "My goodness," she thought. "Children sure speak up a lot more now than they did when mine were young."

The years continued to roll. Marina lived a quiet existence, with her children dropping in to check on her, and grandchildren and great-grandchildren racing in and out. Katie drove in for Thanksgiving one year. She was in college over in Birmingham, Alabama, now. She'd learned to curb her curiosity a little bit, but not much.

November 1978

Marina and Katie ate the traditional turkey feast with Clara's family but were back at the cottage on Olympia Street by early evening. This was the part of the visit both of them had been looking forward to most of all. Outside, a chilly wind blew. Inside, girl and Granny put on their nightgowns. They pulled their chairs close to the propane stove, their hearts all warm and toasty.

Barriers of age dissipated as Marina generously shared her life story. She talked about her girlhood on the edge of the Great Swamp. She shared the memory of a wagon ride on a snowy Christmas Eve and the bitterness of being cheated out of her home. She laughed over the pranks and scrapes of her children and cried over the death of her baby, a loss forty-one years had not been able to ease. Story by story she planted seeds of knowledge that wouldn't mature until long after her own death. Marina shared her wisdom, and the difference in generations became a bridge instead of the gap society claims it must be.

May 1983

Marina continued to tell time by the Farmer's Almanac. Close to twenty-five years had passed since she and Jake had farmed. She was a great-great-grandmother now several times over.

One evening she was walking back into the house after feeding the chickens when the telephone rang. "Hello."

"Hi, Mom. It's Sadie. How are you doin'?"

"Doin' fine, Sadie." It tickled Marina that her children thought they had to identify themselves to her on the phone now that she was close to ninety. There was nothing wrong with her hearing, and she was still the same mother who could distinguish a voice hidden in the cotton field.

"Mom, I need your help."

Marina's full attention focused instantly as she listened for her daughter's words and any unspoken message." What's wrong, Sadie?"

"Well, I've been filling out Social Security paperwork, and I can't find any official document with my full name on it."

"The courthouse should have a copy of your birth certificate."

"I have a copy of my birth certificate. It says only, 'Sadie Hartmann.'"

"What else do you need it to say, Sadie?" Marina asked gently.

"The government wants something that gives my full name, 'Sadie Ophelia Hartmann.' It has to have my middle name."

"Sadie, you don't have a middle name. Your pappy and I never gave you one."

"Well, then where did 'Ophelia' come from?"

"You made it up when you were little. You decided you and Sammy needed middle names and gave them to yourselves."

"Why did you call me 'Sadie Ophelia Hartmann' if I was just plain old 'Sadie Hartmann?'"

"Because you asked me to. You had so much fun thinking up names for yourself and Sammy. I never thought you'd forget you were playing."

"You mean Sammy's name isn't 'Zechariah' either?"

"Of course not! I'd never name my son 'Zechariah!'"

"Does Sammy know he's not 'Samuel Zechariah?'"

Marina began to laugh. "I guess so, but then, I thought you knew you were 'Sadie Hartmann' too."

There was a long sigh at the other end of the phone. "I guess I better get this paperwork done. You need anything, Mommy?"

"No, I don't need a thing."

"All right then," Sadie sighed again, clearly grieving part of her identity. "I'll be down to see you next month."

Marina hung up the phone chuckling. She still never knew what to expect from her children.

. . .

Winter drew close and Marina once again found herself at a gravesite, beyond tired, washed out by emotion. Noel, her gentle-hearted baby brother was gone and buried. How strange that she, the eldest of four, should be the last one living. Even Adele, the aunt who had been like a sister in their girlhood, was now resting under Manila sod. Marina felt empty and wondered if she had lived too long.

Roy offered his arm, but she shook her head. She would walk by herself. Ahead of them on the path, Noel's widow, her sister-in-law Verlena, paused to speak with Mr. Blawton, owner of the land she and Noel had sharecropped. Marina would have preferred to go off the path and leave them their privacy, but Roy steered her straight ahead.

A few more steps and snippets of the conversation reached their ears.

"I'm sorry, Verlena, but I've got crops in the field. I need to get a new sharecropper in there to tend them. I need to move Lowell Harris and his family into the cabin on Sunday so they can start work Monday. You have to move out by Saturday afternoon."

Verlena's troubled face stopped Marina from walking forward. "Saturday?" the bereaved widow exclaimed. "I don't know how I can do that. The dishes and furniture have to be packed. All the tools in Noel's workshop need to be sorted. He never was one for keeping ever'thin' in its place. I was always after him about it."

Inwardly, Marina frowned at the criticism of her brother. She pushed her annoyance aside as Mr. Blawton repeated himself, this time with a firmer voice. "Unfortunately, crops won't wait. We'll need the house emptied by Saturday." The landowner touched his hat as a show of reverence for the dead before doing an abrupt turn and striding off to his car.

Verlena stared after him, slowly processing his commands. "Emptied by Saturday. My girls can help me pack up the house, but where will I go?"

"Can you go with one of your girls?" Marina asked softly.

"Jana doesn't have room. Every inch of her house is full. I suppose Lynnie would take me in, but. . . ." She paused and Marina understood the hesitation. Some generational combinations were more harmonious than others.

Not having an answer, Marina redirected the conversation to a problem with a solution she could arrange. "Roy knows tools well. He can sort through Noel's workshop and pack it up for you.

Verlena's eyes focused on Roy, who nodded his willingness.

"He can start directly after the funeral dinner," Marina stated.

"Or before dinner if you'd like," Roy offered.

"After the funeral dinner will be fine," Marina answered. The living needed to be tended to, but that could happen after due respect had been paid to her brother.

Roy stopped by the next day. "Are you making good progress cleanin' up Noel's workshop?" Marina asked.

"Yes, ma'am." Roy paused, something clearly on his mind. "You're never gonna believe what Uncle Noel had hidden in his workshop."

Marina hesitated, thinking that perhaps the discovery was none of her business.

Roy continued. "Silver dollars! A barrel of silver dollars. I counted them out for Aunt Verlena. Uncle Noel had fourteen thousand silver dollars! Aunt Verlena says it'll buy her a place to live." Roy shook his head. "Mommy, I can't imagine why anyone would collect fourteen thousand silver dollars."

Marina's mind went back to a snowy Christmas Eve seventy years before. She remembered Jake telling a little boy, *whenever you get a silver dollar, you need to hold on to it tight.* She guessed that boy had kept his promise.

Chapter Thirty-Four

July 1984

All the children, the majority of the grandchildren, a good portion of the great-grandchildren, and even a couple of the great-great-grandbabies gathered at Sadie's vacation home on Lake Norfork to celebrate Marina's 90th birthday. Ninety! Marina wondered how that was possible. Even stranger than that, Rosa Lee had turned seventy in May!

To say they had dinner doesn't do the feast justice. Emily baked a ham. Flora brought in chicken, and Hank fried huge platters of Arkansas catfish that had been swimming in the river the day before. His wife brought her own creation—"Sunshine Pie." Potatoes arrived hot, cold, mashed, scalloped, and in salads. Beans simmered and baked. Cousins presented enough casseroles to fill a cookbook. There was a polite competition regarding whose homegrown tomatoes were the best, but it stayed good natured, and all left with the opinions they had arrived with. Watermelons were sliced, chunked, and paired with melons. Desserts had a table and a half all their own. Next to the plates of cookies and brownies, Rosa Lee placed her lemon meringue, chocolate meringue, and (even though it wasn't Thanksgiving) pecan pies. Of course, Marina brought her family-famous coconut cake housed in a Tupperware cake saver. People ate 'til they groaned. Then they sat around and bragged about their misery. It was a meal to tell stories about.

Marina relaxed in a comfortable lawn chair near the picnic table. Bits and pieces of her tribe's conversation floated within her hearing. She loved listening as they updated each other on their jobs and families. Second and third cousins close to the same age reconnected over dessert. In-laws took to the front lawn for a nonstop horseshoe competition. Children scattered to the edges of the property while the youngest mothers tried unsuccessfully to rein them in, but at least they kept them from falling off the side of the mountain.

Emily zipped around the picnic tables, snatching up empty platters, replacing dirty serving spoons, slicing desserts, and cleaning up spills. Watching her, someone asked John, "How do you keep up with her?"

Emily's husband grinned. "I don't try. I just wait for her to come around again."

Across the table a woman with two teenagers detailed the struggles of juggling a career and motherhood. She turned to

Marina. "It's hard to be a working mother, Granny. You don't know about that since you never worked."

Marina thought about choppin' cotton alongside Jake, plantin' and cannin' a garden that fed a family of thirteen, cookin', cleanin', washin', sewin', mendin'. . . .She wondered which part of being a working mother she had missed.

Katie plopped down beside her. She was finished with college, and Marina had attended her wedding the previous summer. "Granny, come to Indiana for Christmas this year," she begged. "We'll have snow. Have you ever had a white Christmas before, Granny?"

Marina nodded. "We used to get a lot more snow in Arkansas than we do now."

"Come anyway. I'll drive down to get you," she coaxed.

"I might do that," Marina responded thoughtfully. "I could have Christmas Eve with Walt and Christmas Day with Flora. It's been over fifty years since I had Christmas with either one of them."

"It's a deal!" Katie kissed her on the forehead and slipped away to find her cousins.

Marina nodded to herself. Flora wanted her to drive back to Indiana with her right after the reunion, but she couldn't get away now. Just imagine what a mess her garden would be in if she took off in the middle of July. The weeds would take over and her vegetables would rot on the ground with no one to can them.

"This place is beautiful, Sadie," Virginia commented. "I don't know how you manage to keep up your home in St. Louis and your property here too."

"Is anything ever out of place?" Clara's daughter-in-law asked.

Sadie laughed and her youngest daughter answered for her. "Never. We swear Mom catches leaves before they hit the ground."

Lilli walked over to the picnic table, chuckling. "Clara's little grandson is over there hidin' behind the garage. He has a whole plate of chocolate chip cookies and is stuffin' cookie after cookie in his mouth just as fast as he can. He saw me lookin' at him and put two in his mouth at once. I guess he was afraid I'd take 'em away from him."

The little guy's mother jumped up from the table and ran to do just that.

Marina remembered her brother Wade doing something similiar when he was about three. Their mother had baked cookies for the preacher who was coming to visit. The preacher was a half hour late and Wade was early. He had eaten half the cookies by the time anyone noticed. Mama sure was mad. Marina smiled at the memory. Funny how clear an incident from eighty-two years ago could be when she didn't remember whether it was last week or the week before that her grandson had come for a visit. Oh, well. What was the difference of a week!

What mattered was that they had time together. That would be important even if she didn't remember the conversation.

Lacy, a granddaughter-in-law, watched Marina soaking up all the activity for a few minutes, then commented, "Poor Granny, living all alone by yourself. I bet you miss havin' people around. After so many years of a full house, isn't it quiet?"

Marina smiled. "Yes, but it's a sweet quiet." How could one resent having time to think?

"They're taking the boats out!" one of the teenagers yelled. Children squealed and began begging their mothers for permission to go.

"I'd like to go for a ride in the boat," Marina stated.

Adult grandchildren glanced at each other in concern. "Do you think that's alright?" "Wouldn't she get sick?" "The boat rocks a lot. I don't know if it's a good idea."

Flora's little Lonnie, now a grandfather, had picked up his boat keys at the house and was walking by the picnic table. "Granny's asking to go for a ride in the boat," someone whispered to him.

Lonnie looked at Marina, who nodded. "I'll take you if you want to go, Granny," he offered.

"That'll be fine." Marina stood up to follow him. Immediately a cloud of relatives surrounded her, ready to guide her down the path to the dock. She sighed. She appreciated the concern, but sometimes so many people helping made it difficult to walk. She wondered if old people's faltering steps were caused by trying to avoid tripping over all the relatives attempting to guide them. Well, they meant well.

Marina stepped down into the boat, hands on all sides reaching out to steady her. "Here, Granny. Sit over here." "This seat has a cushion. Sit here."

Marina grabbed hold of the windshield. "I'll stand right here," she announced.

"Are you sure?" "Have you ever ridden on a boat before?" "The waves can get pretty choppy. I hope you won't get seasick."

Marina smiled to herself. Seasick? Not likely. She had been riding boats at an earlier age than any of them. She still remembered the thrill of duck hunting with her father.

Lonnie steered the boat out into deeper waters. A slight breeze moved through Marina's hair, teasing out memories. She could see another river, another boat. The years disappeared like waves gone to shore.

How strange life was! So often the things you resented brought the best gifts of all. If her family hadn't moved out of the swamps and closer to town after her father died, she never would have met Jake. He and she had built a good life together.

Marina looked at the wooded green mountains as the boat flew past the shore line. She could barely see Sadie's house in the distance now. Who would have thought one of their children would have a beautiful vacation home on top of a mountain? Marina answered her own question. Sadie would have thought so. Sadie had always liked nice things and she was a worker. All of their children were good workers—every one of them. Rosa Lee washed sheets in the basement laundry of a nursing home. Flora and Lilli each had a beauty shop in their home. Walt made good money in the steel mills. Hank ran his own gas station over on the bypass. Roy was a painter who worked for himself. Clara enjoyed being a homemaker. Sammy worked in a factory over in Blytheville. He also hunted and kept her freezer full of meat all winter. Emily and John owned their own farm. Emily was so creative she was always busy with some new craft or sewing project. She was the only one of their children farming now. She and John had expanded their rock house and acreage. They farmed over three hundred acres. Marina and Jake had expected all the children to farm. Well, at least they all put out a good garden every year.

The boat swerved to make the turn back and Marina kept her balance. Yes, they had raised fine children—people who made the world better by being a part of it. Time had tinged Marina's memories with perspective. "We did alright without a house, Jake." She smiled at the recollections. "And we did it without livin' on credit."

Epilogue

Yes, although the names have been changed and the telling fictionalized, these stories are true. Emily did send the cablegram that started John crawling over the Swiss mountains to make it back to her. Sixty-eight years later, he's still crazy in love with her. In spite of their teenage scrapes, Rosa Lee and Flora turned out to be responsible mothers and perfect grandmothers. Hank truly did lead a hospital revolt that rescued his leg, and when Marina's little brother Noel died, thousands of silver dollars really were found in his workshop.

Unfortunately, Eddie was never called into account for his thievery, but he lost more than he gained. He left a worthless inheritance. Despite all our assurances that she had the right to vote, Marina did not ever return to the polls, and to this day, Sadie misses her middle name.

Marina lived the rest of her life in the little bungalow, still planting and harvesting a garden at age ninety-one. Her passing was like the ending of a satisfying book. She died on December

31st as the old year was ebbing away and while Katie was in labor with Marina's great-great-grandson.

Marina's life is the story of loyal love, an insistence on beauty, and the redemption of joy in spite of circumstances. For those of us who loved her, and perhaps that now includes you, her courage, strength, and perseverance continue. As surely as Little River flows to the Mississippi and on to the ocean, her life inspires us.

And always remember — tales told by your elders on the front porch at twilight are a great heirloom.

Author's Note

The town of Manila is tucked into the northeast corner of Arkansas. Marina's house still stands on Olympia Street, not far from the town hall.

The portrait of "Marina" (Mary Parker Crouse) taken at the fair and a photo of "Hank" (Wes Crouse) in uniform are housed at the Manila Museum, which is in the town depot at 100 Dewey Street, Manila, Arkansas. Over one hundred years old, the depot has been renovated to its original state. It hosts antiques, photos, and a treasure of research materials.

Big Lake is a wildlife refuge. Under the care and direction of Jeremy Bennett, the Great Swamp is returning to the wildness of Marina's childhood. You can stand at Timm's Point close to where the Dunkin Ice House was located and look out at the ducks just as she did. A wooden walkway and observation deck overlook the Mud Slough area and Baker's Island. Hunting, while not unlimited the way it was when Papa was a market hunter, is allowed in season.

I'm sure Marina and Jake would welcome you to Mississippi County.

CPSIA information can be obtained at www.ICGtesting.com
Printed in the USA
BVOW05s1801030314

346530BV00002B/2/P

9 781628 399622